WAKE UP AND SMELL THE COFFEE

WAKE UP AND SMELL THE COFFEE

ERIC BOGOSIAN

THEATRE COMMUNICATIONS GROUP/NEW YORK

This publication is made possible in part with public funds from the New York State Council on the Arts, a State Agency.

TCG books are exclusively distributed to the book trade by Consortium Book Sales and Distribution, 1045 Westgate Dr., St. Paul, MN 55114.

LIBRARY OF CONGRESS CATALOGING-IN-PUBLICATION DATA
Bogosian, Eric
Wake up and smell the coffee / by Eric Bogosian.—1st ed.
p.cm.
ISBN 1-55936-202-2 (alk. paper)
1. Success—Drama. 2. Social Classes—Drama. 3. Failure (Psychology)—
Drama. I. Title.

PS3552.O46 W35 2001
812'.54—dc21
2001027318

Book design and typography by Lisa Govan
Cover design by Carin Goldberg and Shigeto Akiyama
Cover illustration by John Howard
Author photo by Joan Marcus

First edition, May 2002

For Amanda

CONTENTS

Wake Up and Smell the Coffee premiered at the Jane Street Theatre in the spring of 2000. Eighteen months later, when this book was scheduled for publication, terrorists attacked New York City and Washington, D.C., killing thousands.

The imagery in these monologues reads very differently now. As I reviewed the material for a final edit, it was painful to scan the line: "A dark day dawns on this American city this morning, a city in mourning this morning . . ."

I feel things now I didn't feel when I wrote those words. I know things now I didn't know then. My thoughts on the bombing in Oklahoma City are different. Airports, flying in planes, is an altogether altered experience. Arabs and Muslims have greater dimension for me now. My personal fear is more tangible. And perhaps, most importantly, my faith in people has changed—ironically I have more faith now.

I considered removing lines or updating references. My strongest impulse was to dump the book altogether. My director Jo Bonney and my editor Terry Nemeth convinced me that the material must stand as written. Ironically, despite the tone of these monologues, they are a product of a more innocent time.

And so, here's *Wake Up and Smell the Coffee*. I no longer perform the piece in its entirety.

Eric Bogosian
New York City
February 2002

ACKNOWLEDGMENTS

I would like to thank folks for making *Wake Up and Smell the Coffee* possible.

First and foremost, Jo Bonney, my collaborator and director, this show belongs to both of us.

Thanks to Arabella Powell, our wonderful stage manager.

To the editors of this edition Terry Nemeth and Kathy Sova, thank you for your extraordinary support and effort.

Thanks to my producers Fred Zollo, Nick Paleologus, Robert Birmingham.

Thanks to George Lane and Ron Taft who keep the water hot.

Thanks to Peter Askin for his beautiful heart and mind.

To Ellen Rusconi, Scott Striegel, and all the folks at the Jane Street Theatre. To the irascible Philip Rinaldi and Barbara Carroll. To John Arnone, Kevin Adams and Don DiNicola who made it look and sound so terrific. To Carin Goldberg, John Howard and Joan Marcus for pretty images. To Kathy Russo and Mary Shimkin at Washington Square Arts who keep my ass moving. To Will Knapp for road support. To Michael Rausch for always being there, no matter what. To Matthew Van Winkle who sorted it all out. And thanks to Performance Space 122 and the Knitting Factory where most of the work was first presented.

Finally, this book is dedicated to Amanda Burroughs Moran my co-worker and bud for the past seven years. Couldn't have done it without you.

Wake Up and Smell the Coffee opened May 4, 2000 at the Jane Street Theatre in New York City. It was directed by Jo Bonney and produced by Frederick Zollo, Nicholas Paleologus, Robert Birmingham and Peter Askin.

WAKE UP AND SMELL THE COFFEE

THE PROMISE

Garrulous, shouting into a mike directly at the audience, menacing:

THANK YOU VERY MUCH. THANK YOU VERY MUCH. LET'S GET ONE THING STRAIGHT. THERE ARE THOSE THAT RULE AND THERE ARE THOSE THAT ARE RULED. THE FUCKERS AND THE FUCKEES. THE MASTERS AND THE SLAVES. THAT'S THE WAY THE WORLD WORKS. THE WINNERS, THE LOSERS, THE KILLERS AND THE DEAD. AND I AM THE TOP DOG. AND DOG SPELT BACKWARDS IS GOD.

THOSE WHO WANT TO FUCK WITH ME, I GOT ONE WORD FOR YOU: *PAIN.* YOU DON'T LIKE PAIN, DON'T GET IN THE RING WITH ME. 'CAUSE I'LL BREAK EVERY BONE IN YOUR BODY. JUST TROT DOWN TO THE LOCKER ROOM AND HAVE A TEARFUL LITTLE SHOWER. IF YOU DO LIKE PAIN, YOU KNOW WHERE TO FIND ME . . . 'CAUSE I'M THE DOG ON TOP!

(Slams down the mike stand. Pause. Then gently into the mike:)

THANK YOU.

INTRO

Lights up. He slips on a black sports jacket and walks toward the audience.

Thank you, thank you. Thanks so much for coming by. I really appreciate it.

Tonight we're going on a journey. This theatre is our ship and I'm your captain. Hopefully, you're going to see things from a slightly different perspective, gain a little insight, renew your empathy.

And we're going to have some fun too. I'm gonna give you that Lenny-Bruce-esque experience that transforms tragedy into comedy. That turns it all upside-down and cuts through the bullshit and the hypocrisy.

Because that's what theatre is all about, isn't it? Insight into human nature. And with that insight comes understanding; with understanding—action; and from action, change and a better world.

Sure, I'm just one guy up here. And let's face it, you're pretty much a room full of strangers. But tonight, tonight we become as one. Tonight we're not just separate individuals, islands, lonely and adrift. Tonight we are like snowflakes in a storm, swirling together, each one of us unique, but also part of something much larger, each one of us a frozen droplet of potential.

As we swirl together tonight, who knows where we might end up? We are limited only by our imagination! Perhaps as a snowdrift high upon a mountain peak! Perhaps the highest mountain—Mount Everest! Why not?

We fall gently, one upon the other, one flake upon his fellow flake, immobile, caught in the frozen silence of the Himalayas.

Until one day, the sun warms us and we melt. We become a trickle, the trickle becomes a stream, the stream a river, as we reunite with all the other little drops and become a mighty torrent. Powerful, roaring, cascading—we are the *Ganges*—yes! Immense, pouring down into the valley. Full of life and energy and *fish*! People are swimming in us! Bathing in us! Laughing, joking!!!

Elephants squirt arcing sprays from their trunks! Shamans baptize their followers in our sacred waters! Dark-eyed women scrub their washing on the rocks, pounding their dhotis and saris with sticks, the water droplets splashing joyously up into the air! Even the dead are brought to us upon their fiery funeral pyres, as they say their final good-bye to this transient life. People chant! They sing! They celebrate! We are the river, we are life itself! We are HOLY!

(Pause.)

Wow. All that right here in this theatre, tonight.

And so, hopefully, if my humble little show touches you in any way, if I do manage to reach out and communicate to just a few of you, an incremental change may come over you and you might walk out of this theatre a slightly different person.

You'll walk out of here and who knows what you might do? Maybe you'll write that letter to your mother your therapist has been telling you to write. Break up with that boyfriend who's been vegetating for the last six months. Lose ten pounds. Throw away those cigarettes for good. Give someone a hug.

Or write a novel. A play. A screenplay!

Inspired, you just might invent something, some great new invention—penicillin! Well, they've already invented penicillin, but something like penicillin. Something that changes the lives of millions. That changes the course of history!

(Pause. Looks the audience straight into the eyes, brimming with optimism, then:)

Or not. Maybe none of that will happen. Maybe you'll just walk out of this theatre, and enjoy nothing more than a pathetic wordless ride home, you realizing that, despite my every effort up here on your behalf, *nothing* has changed, there has been no progress in your life whatsoever. And indeed you will go home and set the alarm clock one more time, knowing full well that you're going to get up tomorrow morning, same as every morning, and go back to that same God-forsaken job you hate with every molecule of your being. And everyone of those misfits you've endured for the past five, ten, fifteen years, will be there tomorrow, same as yesterday, same as today and there's *nothing* you can do about it.

You are locked in an endless cycle of conformity, a grinding featureless routine, punctuated by only the most lame and insipid diversions, of which *this* is obviously one.

And I want to tell you, I relate. I identify. I do. I feel your pain. And it hurts. It hurts a lot. And I want to help. But I can't help. There's not much I can do about it from this vantage point.

I don't have any answers. I don't have any "message." I can't make you *think* unless you were already thinking before you came by the theatre. Which is a fifty-fifty proposition. All I can do up here is distract you for about seventy-five minutes. Make you *numb*, sedate you. Make painless this unending trail of shit we call a life. This tar pit of stupidity, this vat of spiritual oatmeal, this slimy snail track of frustration, this pointless, stupid, mosh pit of fuckwits and hypocrites and pinheads with whom we must *cohabit* like ants on an anthill, like crabs in a bottle, like bacterium in a dirty drop of water, endlessly fighting and competing, fighting and competing, fighting and competing, consuming and shitting. Like food tubes with absolutely no purpose whatsoever.

Let's be honest. You'll sit here tonight, watch the show, leave, shove an ice-cream cone down your throat, and come tomorrow morning this show, like that ice cream, will be nothing more than a vague memory, flushed away and forgotten.

I don't know why I waste my breath. Because everybody knows, everybody knows what I'm saying, but everybody pretends not to know. It's mass delusional self-hypnosis. It's meaningless. Really. C'mon! Communication? Inspiration? Insight? Bullshit.

If I had any guts at all, I'd walk off this stage right now. *(Walks offstage; from off)* I'd walk off and I wouldn't come back. *(Returns)* But I don't have any guts. And I need the check.

OK. OK. OK. You want insight into human nature? OK, here's some insight into human nature. Let's play a little game, we'll call it: "The Insight into Human Nature Game"!

No, that's a lousy name for a game. Here's a much better name. We'll call it: "Who Wants to Be a Millionaire?" But we won't play the TV version, that's bull. Let's play it the way it's really played in the real world. "Who Wants to Be a Millionaire?"

(He jumps over to the mike, and speaks in an announcer voice:)

OK, contestants! You know the rules! There's a little button in front of each one of you. Push the button and one million dollars tax-free is instantly deposited in a Swiss bank account in your name. But don't forget when you push that button, millions of people will also be instantly thrown out of work and spend the rest of their lives in abject poverty and misery.

(He drops the voice and steps back toward the audience.)

Question: How long do you *wait* before you push the button? Or let's bring it right here, right now. There's a button in front of each one of you. You push the button and I go up in a big ball of flame. And I die, writhing in agony, right before your eyes.

Question: Do you push the button, or do you just wait for the person sitting next to you to push the button?

(Youthful voice:)

Yeah we went to this show, man, and it was kind of interesting. There was this guy on stage talking about something, I'm not sure what, and then he just went whoosh and went up in a ball of fire! Turned all black and wrinkled-up and crusty like a piece of chicken you leave on the barbecue for too long. It was awesome! *(Catches himself)* I mean it was disturbing too, you know. It really made me think.

(Switches back to normal voice:)

C'mon, admit it. Wouldn't you love it if I just dropped dead up here right now? Wouldn't that be a unique experience? Right? You don't really know me, why should you care? You could dine out on that one for the next six months: "I was there, man." You could email your best friend: "Went to this show, guy died on stage. It was . . . it was disturbing. Really made me think."

If you think there's any level of compassion or empathy or civilization whatsoever being shared out there by anybody, I got news for you, there is none. Wake up and smell the coffee, it's anarchy. It's chaos barely being held together by pious hypocrisy and gross sentimentality.

The blind leading the blind. No, that's not right, it's the *retarded* leading the blind. *(Forrest Gump voice)* "Life is like a box of chocolates. You never know what you're going to get." Great moments in Western civilization! I have to write that one down. Never thought of things that way before:

"You never know what you're going to get"! Deep! A hero for our times. *(Sling Blade voice)* "SOME CALL IT A SLING BLADE." Great retard, Billy Bob. Will somebody please give that man an Oscar? "Some call it a sling blade." *(Dustin Hoffman Rain Man voice and posture)* "Eighty-two, eighty-two, eighty-two. Two hundred and forty-*six*, two hundred and forty-six toothpicks in the box, Raymond."

(Drops to his knees, pleading to the audience:)

WE'RE DOWN HERE LOOKING UP AT THE MENTALLY HANDICAPPED. WHERE DOES THAT PUT US???? RIGHT IN THE ESPRESSO BAR WITH A TATTOO AND A CELL PHONE, THAT'S WHERE!

(Jumps back into Forrest Gump:)

"Life is like a box of chocolates, you never know what you're going to . . ." I KNOW WHAT I'M GOING TO GET, I KNOW WHAT I'M GOING TO GET: I'M GONNA GET *FUCKED*. THAT'S WHAT I'M GOING TO GET!

VOICE IN THE WILDERNESS

Rushes to a chair and faces upstage as if watching the performance. Whiny, older theatre-goer voice:

What's this show about anyway? What is this? What are you talking about up there? What happened to the journey down the river? I was looking forward to that part. You came out, you were saying life was beautiful and how theatre was about insight and communication and I thought, It won't be *Vagina Monologues*, but I'll be moved. I want to be moved! I want catharsis when I go to the theatre!

Instead you come out and you're swearing and negative. *Very* negative. I spent the whole afternoon at the yoga center getting rid of all my stress. I come by here to see a nice piece of theatre and now my neck hurts . . . just by listening to you for five minutes. What are you saying, we should all kill ourselves? Is that what you're saying? And let me ask you something, what's the deal with your hair? Is that your real hair? Or do you have that done?

You know what your problem is? You're too negative. You know why you're so negative? You're full of *fear*. My therapist told me that, cost me a hundred and fifty bucks. I'll give it to you gratis. You're full of *fear*. Because you have no spirituality. You don't believe in anything. You need to have more faith!

FAITH

Leaps out of chair; addresses the "theatregoer" in the chair:

"FAITH"? You mean "faith" like faith in my government?

(Swivels and mimes firing two handguns at an invisible assailant.)

WATCH OUT! HE'S GOT A GUN! *(Mimes shooting)* BOOM, BOOM, BOOM, BOOM!!! *(Trots forward)* I THINK HE'S GOT A GUN! *(Mimes shooting)* BOOM, BOOM, BOOM, BOOM!!! *(Stands over the "fallen target")* I'M PRETTY SURE HE'S GOT A GUN! *(Mimes shooting at prone figure)* BOOM, BOOM, BOOM, BOOM!!! *(Stands over the "body," kicks something out of the way. Looks up, distracted)* Never mind!

(Addresses "theatregoer" in chair again:)

Or maybe you mean faith in the goodness of mankind? I'll have to take a trip over to Chechnya or Bosnia or Rwanda and refresh my memory of how wonderful people can be to their fellow man. I'll pick up a femur, keep it on my mantelpiece to remind myself of human nature.

No, you don't mean any of that do you? You must mean faith in God! Right? Is that what you mean? Faith in a "higher power" as we say these days.

(Turns away from chair and addresses the audience:)

13

Well, let me tell you something: *my* God—I believe in God—*my* God is a capricious little fucker. Or should I say "big fucker"? I mean, here's a guy—we're all clear here on who God is, right? The most powerful being in the universe! Has to be, if He weren't, if there were some other being more powerful than Him, well then . . . he'd be God wouldn't he?

My God is all powerful. He can do anything. My God could feed every hungry person on the planet Earth—like that *(Snaps fingers)*—tomorrow! He could rid the world of disease—like that. All those little bald children on the Cancer Channel? Gone, healthy, in great shape! *(Snaps fingers)* God could do that.

He could give us an extra hour of sunshine every day. Create a few more parking spaces. But noooooo! That would be too easy. He doesn't want to do *that*! No, my God doesn't like to do the easy stuff, it's boring to Him. He doesn't want to do what everybody wants Him to do. Kind of like Lou Reed, He does what He wants to do. He's got integrity. He's not going to sell out.

So, anyway, my God is hanging around heaven one day, two thousand years ago, getting a little antsy, and decides to take a trip down to Palestine, starts hanging out with this Jewish chick named Mary. Right? Kind of a weird name for a Jewish girl. But anyway, they get busy and the next thing you know, she's knocked-up, pregnant. Nobody's even sure how He did it. Kind of a theological question: does God have a dick? If He does, how *big* is it? How many angels can dance on the head of it? We don't have to answer that question tonight.

And they have this kid, baby Jesus. Not just any kid, God's *only* son. God isn't like some kind of NBA player that has a kid in every town. This is God's *only* son, the only son of God. *(Aside to the audience, if such a thing is possible in a direct address)* By the way, I'm not making any of this up, it's all in the Bible, you can read it when you get home.

So what does God do with His *only* son? Does He take him to a ball game? Teach him how to fish? Read him the Sunday comics? No, He has him tortured to *death*. Takes this poor guy. This meek, little, skinny Jewish carpenter. Nice guy, sweet guy, looks just like Willem Dafoe. With the little *Home Improvement* carpenter belt, little hammer and everything. Has these Roman soldiers march this poor little guy all over town in his underwear, whipping him, sticking things in his side, the sponge with vinegar (which I never got), giving him a hard time, crown of thorns on his head, the whole nine yards. Terrible. Dragging this huge piece of lumber on his back. How ironic, he's a *carpenter*.

They drag him up on top of this hill, nail his hands to the wood. Can you imagine what that felt like! You ever get a paper cut? How much that hurts? *NAILS!* I mean, who thinks this stuff up? *Daddy*, that's who! *(God voice)* "Just use one nail on the feet, I'm building a shed behind heaven, I don't want to waste the hardware."

(Strikes a crucifixion pose, arms out, head tilted, looking upward.)

And Jesus's hanging there in the sun, cooking, blood dripping. His abandonment issues are kicking up. His inner child feels like shit. He's got some issues with his dad. So he looks up to heaven and says, *(In a California surfer voice)* "Like, Dad? Yo, can I ask you a question?" *(Contemplates one nailed hand, then the other)* "Are you pissed off at me about something? Because I've been really good, you know? I've done everything you asked me to. Did all the weddings and the bar mitzvahs. Hung out with those twelve deadbeats. And they never pick up a check, Dad, *never*. Walked on water. And then you wanted me to go out in the desert and I did it. Said don't eat anything and I didn't. Don't drink and, Dad, you can get real thirsty in the desert. And then Satan came and tried to tempt me with like chicks and money and he even said he could get my film into Sundance and I said, 'NO! Get thee behind me, Satan-dude. Uh-uh, not interested, because I'm with the Big Guy.'" *(Points upward, pulling at his nail)* "Owww! 'I'm with the guy upstairs, I'm with *DADDY!*'"

(Jumps off "cross"; preaches in a Holy Roller voice, very animated:)

BECAUSE HE *BELIEVED*! HE BELIEVED THAT THE GOOD LORD WOULD *PROTECT* HIM. HE BELIEVED THE ALMIGHTY LORD WOULD TAKE HIM INTO HIS ALL-POWERFUL ARMS AND SHELTER HIM. HE BELIEVED THAT THE GOOD LORD WOULD TAKE CARE OF HIS LITTLE SHEEP! HE HAD *FAITH, FAITH, FAITH*!!!

(Switches back to normal voice:)

. . . So, what happens? The old man in the sky, *Daddy*, took little Jesus, His son, nailed his skinny butt to a piece of wood in the middle of the desert so a bunch of jerk-offs could check him out like some kind of rotisserie chicken at the Safeway.

Now the only reason I bring all this up, and this is kind of the long way around to make a point, but dig, this is what God does to His *own kid*. You really think He's going to get all stretched out of shape worrying about *your* anonymous ass? I doubt it. I doubt it *sincerely*.

You want me to have faith? I have faith. I have faith that *shit happens*. Really, really bad . . .

ARABS

Face changes expression as if witnessing some horrible event on the horizon over the audience's heads. Redneck voice:

OH MY GOD, NO! THEY JUST BLEW THAT BUILDING UP IN OKLAHOMA CITY! THAT'S THE WORST THING I EVER SEEN IN MY LIFE! HUNDREDS OF PEOPLE KILLED! LITTLE CHILDREN! WHO COULD A DONE SOMETHIN' LIKE THAT? *(Realizing)* MUST A BEEN ONE OF THOSE ARAB TERRORISTS! SURE IT WAS! ONE OF THOSE A-RABS. LOTS OF A-RABS OUT HERE IN OKLAHOMA CITY! YEAH IT WAS ONE OF THEM ARABS ALL RIGHT. ONE OF THEM BUSHY-HAIRED, BEADY-EYED, BIG-NOSED, BLACK-BEARDED, TOWEL-HEADED, OILY-SKINNED, SMELLY, GOAT-FUCKING, MOHAMMED-LOVING A-AS-IN-ASSHOLE-ARABS. *(Gesticulating, miming)* WHY WHEN WE GET A HOLD THAT SAND NIGGER, WE'RE GONNA SHOVE A POSEIDON MISSLE RIGHT UP HIS CRACK, TEACH HIM *YOU DON'T FUCK WITH THE U.S. of A*!!!!
(Cocks his head) Wait! What's that? Not an Arab? Blond hair? Blue eyes? Loves Kenny G? Shit, well, he must be misguided then. We have to learn to understand and forgive. But you're right, right! He killed all those little kids, and many of whom were white. We're gonna have ta lynch him! Come 'ere you Timothy McVeigh! Quick where's a rope? Where's a tree? Where are the TV cameras? This is America—can't do this without a TV camera. Where's an anchorman, where's that Bernard Shaw guy?

(Bursts into operatic voice à la My Fair Lady:*)*

The rain in Spain
Falls mainly on the plain . . .
La-la-la-la-la!!!

(Switches back to redneck voice:)

NO, NOT THAT ONE, YOU DICK! THE CNN ONE!
WHERE IS HE? IN KOSOVO? WHERE THE HELL IS
KOSOVO? WELL, WE NEED AN ANCHORMAN! YOU,
YOU'RE AN ANCHORMAN, GET UP THERE, LET'S GET
THIS SHOW ON THE ROAD! *(Counts down with his fingers,
facing the upstage mike on its stand)* FIVE, FOUR, THREE,
TWO, ONE! YOU'RE ON!

*(Runs over and gets behind the mike, switches to anchorman
voice, speaking calmly and directly to the audience:)*

A dark day dawns on this American city this morning. A city
in mourning . . . this morning. What forces seek to disrupt
our cherished American beliefs of love, peace and justice? A
tragedy. Children were killed. Why? Who knows? Some
lunatic got "pissed off." A veteran? Perhaps, let's not think
about that too much, it hurts to think. Let's think instead of
our president's words just this morning:

(Switches to Bill Clinton voice, almost cheerful, eyes twinkling:)

This is a terrible thing. We are so sad today. We will find the
motherfucker who did this and we will kill him as slowly and
painfully as possible.

(Anchorman voice:)

Today, as we feel this tragedy, let's feel all the tragedies. Let's think about crack babies and homeless people and starving Africans. And let's cry. Let's all have a good cry. For them and even more so, for ourselves. Because we feel their pain, because we know their pain, because we want their pain to go away so we don't have to hear about it anymore. Thank you, good night. And remember that tonight's Oklahoma City bombing coverage will preempt the previously scheduled documentary: "Hiroshima: The Little Nips Got What They Deserved," or "Hiroshima: If They're Not White, It's Not Terrorism," or "Hiroshima: Thirty Thousand Is Not Really That Many People When You Consider the Alternative," or . . . And now a word from our sponsor:

THE OFFER

Easygoing, sipping from a mug of coffee.

Do you feel like life is passing you by? Do you get up in the morning and ask yourself, "What's it all about anyway?" And what's your answer? Prozac? Viagra? Suicide? Hi, I'm Satan and I'm here to tell you there's a much better solution.

What do you want out of life? Money, power, sex? How about guns? Drugs? Fireworks? You can have it all. But why stop there? People come in and say, "I want to have sex with my secretary." Come on! Use your imagination! How about sex with your *grandmother*? Sex with your neighbor's *dog*? Sex with your own *kids*? The sky's the limit. What have you got to lose? Your *soul*? Hell, when was the last time you even knew you had one?

Time to stop *denying* yourself. Time to start doing *all* those things you *always* wanted to do! And I'm not just talking about smoking crack and chowing down on Krispy Kreme doughnuts. I've got clients out there today, doing really creative things like firebombing helpless villages, stockpiling anthrax, rigging election ballots. Why should the big boys have all the fun?

So many millions of miserable people are out there not overeating, not smoking, not drinking, not masturbating! No wonder you're all so depressed. And why? To be good? Because "God's watching you"? I got a little secret I'll let you in on: God's got better things to do than watch you play with your pee-pee.

You know, I was checking out that plane that crashed in the Rocky Mountains last week. Three hundred people dead. Boom! Like that. Body parts all over the snow. It was awesome. And all I could think was, I wonder how many of them were on a diet? How many were trying to stop smoking? Hey, they're smokin' now baby!

Only one thing I can't get you and that's *peace of mind.* It's not my thing. I honestly think it's overrated. All these people trying to chill out and calm down and be serene. You'll have plenty of time to be serene when you're six feet under in a box. You want serenity, you gotta go to those other guys, Jesus and Buddha. See what that gets you. A REALLY BORING LIFE. But what do I know, I've only been in business for over five thousand years! Fuck me.

So come on down and sign on the dotted line, you *know* you want to. We're here for you, twenty-four-seven/three-sixty-five. Especially Christmas and Easter. Time to start living!

THE AIRPORT

Addresses the audience:

So I'm in the airport the other day. It's a special experience going to an airport these days. It's pretty much a paradigm for life as we know it today. There are only two modes: running and waiting. You know the drill, you've all been to the airport. Hundreds, thousands of people. Running, waiting. Or some variation thereof: running to wait, waiting to run. Standing in ticket lines, sitting in the departure lounge, crowded around the baggage carousel watching the luggage coming out as if awaiting the birth of your first child: "Oooooh! Look, look! Here it comes!" Washing and flushing in the smelly restrooms. They never stop cleaning the bathrooms at the airport. Trying to take a leak while some guy mops around your feet. *(Miming harried pisser)* "Just a sec, just a sec!!!" *(Hops from one foot to the next, still holding onto his dick)* "How's that?"

Drinking in the bar area, sitting on those ugly bent chrome-and-naugahyde stools watching the drop-down color TV, watching live coverage of plane crashes from around the world. Snacking in the snack area, being served by the sullen Mexicans and Pakistanis shoveling out the tacos and nachos and hot dogs and doughnuts and pizza. Chewing furiously like rodents before dragging their dirty little spoiled children from Cleveland to Orlando to Denver to Philly to L.A.

(Starts running in circles, illustrating:)

23

Running to wait. Waiting to run. Faster and faster. Hot decaf lattes sloshing out of the cups scalding their hands. Beepers beeping. Overweight garment bags ripping the muscle and sinew from their shoulder bones. John Grisham novel tucked safely under their arm. Cell phones to their ears.

(Removes cell phone from jacket pocket and puts it to his ear as he finds a spot in line:)

GOLD CARD

Talking into cell phone, harried nasal businessman:

Jerry, yeah, hey it's me. I'm at the airport. Oh, they delayed my flight and they're gonna stick us on another plane. No, no problem, I've got the gold card. Just a sec, Jerry, someone's asking me something. *(Turning, putting the phone to his chest)* This is the gold card line, do you have a gold card? *(Reveals gold card from pocket)* One of these? You don't have a gold card? See that long line runs all the way down through the terminal? That's your line. No, I don't know where you get one. Sorry. Good luck! Have a nice flight! *(Returns to call)* Jerry? Yeah, so, no, things are very mellow. I've been taking this meditation course. It's great, only takes thirty seconds a day, and the best part is, you can be doing something else at the same time! And me and the fam just got back from vacation, man! Oh, yeah, kind of a *working vacation.* Pittsburgh! In the morning I'd see clients and then in the afternoon we went sightseeing, visited coal mines. *(Checks watch)* So listen, Jerry, I just wanted to call to say they're keeping me out in L.A. through the weekend, so gonna have to scratch the golf date. Yeah. So how's next week? No? Uh, week after that's no good for me. And next month I've got the convention in Chicago. Then I hit Detroit, Osaka, Tampa, Vancouver, Mexico City and Ulan Bator. Then after that is my busy period.

Well, hey look, we'll get together sooner or later. We're best friends aren't we? Look, Jerry, why don't I call you, say,

in two months, how's that sound? And hey it was great getting together with you last year. Sorry I had to leave a little
early, I had a client in town. OK! Yeah, me too, I gotta go too.
Yeah. Cool. OK. Say hi to Janey. Judy, Judy, right.

*(Starts to dial again, then notices someone cutting ahead in
the line.)*

Excuse me? Sir? Excuse me! This is a line here. We're standing in line. *(Pause)* I know you have a gold card, we *all* have
gold cards in this line. This isn't some new age party game, it's
a line. *(Pause)* Oh, OK, no problem, an honest mistake. *(His eyes
follow the interloper making his way to the back of the line,
past him)* I'm curious though, you came in here, you saw all
these people standing in line and you thought—what?—Oh,
look at all those people standing in line. I'll just cut in front
of them, fuck them.

Hey, you know what? *FUCK YOU! (Pause)* Watch my language? Watch my language? You walk in here, treat me like
shit on your shoe and you want me to watch my language?
You know what you are, pal? You're the kind of person when
they have those soccer games in Europe a riot breaks out and
everybody's rushing for the gates, you're the one who steps
on some baby's windpipe.

No, no. You know who you are? You're the kind of person
who, when a plane crashes in the Andes and the survivors
are freezing and starving to death, you're the guy who starts
chewing on someone's leg!

But why should you care what I have to say? You're never
going to see me again. I'm nothing to you. Just one more
anonymous human being in your way. I could drop dead at
your feet right now, and you'd just step right over me: "Oh
lucky day, an extra space in line!"

(Dials the phone again, but then can't help himself; he turns.)

You know what you are? You're everything that's wrong with the world today. Nobody respects anybody else anymore. Nobody wants to participate in civilization. That's what this is. This line, this line of ten people standing here is civilization. And *you* are the Dark Ages, pal. You are the barbaric hordes coming *down*. That's what you are. You are the Mongols, the Huns, the Visigoths, the Turks. Why don't you just get a sword and chop us all to pieces? Then there'd be no one ahead of you. You could stick our heads on poles. Maybe send us to a camp someplace. Yeah, just go stand in that line! That's not the gold card line. *(To phone)* Sonia? Hello, honey? Oh, honey, it's Daddy, Jeremy, is Mommy there? Get Mommy. Daddy. Daddy. DADDY! The guy who lives in your house. Listen, can you get Mommy, I'm at the airport. And it's an emergency and I have to talk to Mommy right now. *(Impatient, but talking in a slight babyish tone)* Yes. That's right. Daddy's going to fly in a big airplane. No, no I don't think so, it's not going to go "BOOM" and crash. That wouldn't be nice, now would it? Get Mommy please. Huh? Of course I'm gonna get you something. Don't I always get you something? I don't know, something. Yes. It'll be worth at least twenty dollars, yes. Please get Mommy. Get Mommy now.

(Pause.)

Hello? Hello? Sonia! Why are you letting him pick up the phone? What if it were an emergency—the plane was about to crash and I want to tell you how much I love you and I'm explaining the meaning of life to a six year old? *(Speaking more and more rapidly)* Well, I don't know, they canceled the flight and they're moving me from line to line and the battery on the laptop went down and I'm fibrillating from all the cappuccinos I've been drinking. Well, I don't know what they did before laptops, I'm just saying . . . Oh, you'll never guess who just came into the lounge. Here! Here! *(Covers the cell*

phone not to be overheard, whispering) Calista Flockhart!
I can't say it any louder than that. *(Again covers the phone,
almost unintelligible)* Calista Flockhart! *(Out loud, figuring it
out, in awe)* We must be on the same flight! We'll be breath-
ing the same air molecules all the way to Los Angeles!!! Wow.
Do you think she'd think I'm an asshole if I asked her for her
autograph? Wait, what's the name of her TV show? Come on,
Sonia, this is important! Listen, call my sister in Buffalo, ask
her what's the name of the show that *(Whispering)* Calista
Flockhart *(Normal)* is on—she knows these things. Put it on
my voicemail, I'll check in later from the plane. Just do it,
OK? For Jeremy, please?

Oh shit, they're calling me for the flight. So listen, the reason I called is I'm not coming home tomorrow, they're gonna
hold me out there until Monday for meetings. I know. I know
it's our anniversary but . . . of course, I don't have to. I can
come home right now if I want. Do you want me to come
home? You want me to come home? *(High-pitched)* I'll come
home right now. I won't have a job, but I can come home.
I don't need this job. I'll just stay home, we'll make tie-dye
T-shirts, candles, macramé.

Honey, honey, don't say that. We have lots of quality time
together. Of course we do. What about Pittsburgh? You got to
wear that neat hat with the little light in the front. Oh, now
you're crying, come on!

Honey, listen, I promise when I get back, we'll take the
frequent flyer miles and we'll go somewhere really nice.
Someplace expensive. With a spa. Yes. With massages, yes.
Facials. I don't know if they'll have liposuction, I don't have
the brochure with me. Listen, honey, let me get on the plane,
I'll call you from the plane. *(Starts to move toward the gate)*
Listen . . . Sonia, the next time you feel bad about us always
being apart, just imagine this: you and me, together all the
time, working a doubleshift at a McDonald's . . . I gotta go.
OK, alright, OK, alright, I love you too.

UPGRADE

Perky and patronizing:

Here you go, sir, you're all set. You have a seat on this flight, it's leaving in ten minutes so you better hurry up! Yes, sir, that's right, it's a coach seat. Yes, I know you had a fully-paid-for-first-class ticket, sir, but this seat is coach. Well, let me see what I can do, OK? *(Types into keyboard)* Alright, I'm looking at a first-class seat on a 3:30 A.M. departure with a six-hour layover in Saint Louis. How's that sound?

Yes, 3:30 in the morning, sir, that's correct. I understand that, sir. Yes, I can see that you have a gold card. All the people behind you have gold cards, sir. Well, sir, sir, sir, why don't we do this: step aside for a sec here, let me get everyone on board, get them seated, let the flight leave and then we can see what we can do, OK? *(Signals to next person)* Next in line?

I'm not trying to get rid of you, sir. Our gold card passengers are our first priority. Would you like a voucher for a complimentary cup of Starbucks coffee while you wait? Sir! Sir! Sir! There's no reason to use that language. May I remind you, sir, that we are being videotaped as we speak and this videotape is admissible as evidence in any court proceedings that may arise from our conversation on this date.

Well, I'm sorry you feel that way. Yes, you may file a complaint. Just get in touch with our operations manager. He's not in right now, but if you'd like to drop by tomorrow morning around seven A.M., I'm sure he'd love to see you.

You can't, sir, no. No, you can't sue us, sir. Well if you read the notice on the back of your ticket you will see that it says that when you fly with us you agree to abide by all the rules and regulations of this airline and any disagreements you have with the rules and regulations of this airline are subject to arbitration by an independent arbitrator. OK?

You *can* win, sir. You can win. You just can't win *today*. Have a nice flight! Next!

HARMONIOUS

Speaking in a British/Indian accent, deep and resonant with a slight lisp:

Thank you so much for joining me tonight on this journey of spiritual recovery. Let me remind each and every one of you in this room that you are full of energy. With this energy, each of us can change our lives. Together we can change the world.

The first thing you must understand in order to harness this energy is that *you are nothing.* You do not exist. There is no "you." You are only a temporary vessel for the use of the universe to make manifest this moment and this time. You are merely one stitch in the vast carpet of the cosmos. You are no more than one grain of sand in the endless Sahara of the universe. You are one hair on the butt of the hairy gorilla.

The second thing you must understand is that we exist in two states. We are either in sync with the universe or we are out of sync with the universe. When we are in sync with the universe, we call this being *harmonious.* When we are out of sync with the universe, we call this being *alienated.*

We are either in sync or out of sync, harmonious or alienated. How do we know which state we are in? *(Pause, smiles, shrugs shoulders)* We just know!

So let us now clear our minds and still our centers. And let us contemplate these two states of being—harmony and alienation:

I am warm, I am happy, I am harmonious.
I am cold, I am angry, I am alienated.

I am swimming in my heated swimming pool. I am
   harmonious.
I am doing my taxes. I am alienated.
I am buying a brand-new Lexus with all-leather interi-
   or. I am harmonious.
I am working three jobs to pay for health insurance.
   I am alienated.
I am flying first class to Saint Bart's. I am harmonious.
I am going to jail for food stamp fraud. I am alienated.

If we carefully meditate upon these two states of being, we
find a deep and abiding spiritual principle becomes obvious:

Alienation is simply a lack of money.

And, of course, the corollary:

Money brings deep and abiding harmony.

When we have money, our days are full of sunshine, the air
is fresh and clean. We love everyone we meet. And everyone
loves us.

When we lack money, we become empty and angry. We listen to overly loud music. And we are frequently constipated.

And so each and every one of us is on a path and must
answer the eternal question: "How do I get more money?"
This is the path that I am on. That is why you are here tonight.

The paradox of life is . . . paradoxical. In order to breathe
in, we must first breathe out. In order to grasp, we must first
let go. In order for the sun to rise, it must first set. In order to
take what I have to give you, you must first give me two
thousand dollars in four easy installments.

Life surrounds us with an endless bounty. An overflowing
cornucopia of goods and services. They are all there for our
taking. We only have to pay for them. Thank you.

(Puts hands together in prayer and bows silently.)

BREAKTHROUGH

Grabs the upstage chair and moves it downstage slightly. Speaks in a thick workingman's accent. As he sits:

I had a pretty good week this week. Constructive. Constructive. I've been thinking about what you were saying last week about, you know, putting things on the shelf and how I've got to learn how to love myself today, because if I don't, who will? Like you say, "I'm not a human being trying to be spiritual, I'm a spiritual being trying to be human."

I saw my ex.

Picking up the kids.

Total pain in the ass. As usual. Oh yeah. Oh yeah. You know she still blames me for the breakup. It was all my fault everything got fucked-up. Hey, if she had kept a better eye on things and not let me stay out every night till four in the morning but no, that had nothing to do with *her*. When I was there getting arrested and wrecking the car, did she ever think, Maybe this is a cry for help? You know, I'd be in the kitchen, seven A.M., puking my brains out, and she'd be getting the kids ready for school and she'd act like I wasn't even there. Completely ignore me. Did she ever stop to think, Poor guy. Why is he doing this to himself? How can I help him? No, she's a completely self-obsessed human being, out of touch with her feelings. I had to live with that all those years.

Well, I took the boys to the ball game. Oh yeah, it was fun. They're so great. Acting up, throwin' Cracker Jacks at each other. Yelling, screaming. And I'm like, "Hey! Hey! Hey!

Quiet the fuck DOWN! RIGHT NOW!" I'm so good with those guys, you know? Oh! Oh! And this busybody behind me is like, "Stop yelling at your kids, I'm trying to hear the game." And I'm dealing with boundary issues today, like we've been working on, so I'm like, "Are these *your* kids? Or are these *my* kids?" Right? "You don't hear me telling you to put a bag on your wife's head 'cause she's so fuckin' ugly."

And from this, the guy gets an attitude. You know? All indignant. Gets in my face. Now I'm in a fight. How did this happen? And I can walk away, I can walk away. But I have my needs today. And I've learned to respect my needs. And my need was to punch him in the face, so I did.

So yeah, we got thrown out of the stadium. But you know, shit happens, I understand that today. I take life on life's terms. They give you lemons, you make lemonade.

The kids don't always understand. The little one was like, "Why were there only four innings in the game, Daddy?" *(Laughs)* They're so cute. And they want the pennants and the key chains and the baseball caps. And I'm honest with them, you know? "Sorry guys, Daddy doesn't have any money. OK? Daddy doesn't have a job, OK? It's not Daddy's fault he has a dick-head boss who can't take a little honest criticism."

And the little one's like, "I want a Derek Jeter autographed baseball, I want a Derek Jeter autographed baseball." Like a broken record. And I'm like, "You want a Derek Jeter autographed baseball? Go ask Derek Jeter! He's probably got baseballs lying all over his house."

So now *he's* crying. And I'm guilty. I want to kill myself, right there. I even said to them, "You know what? You kids piss me off so much I'm going to jump in front of that subway train, right? Get sliced right in half. Then you'll be happy. Just like your mother!" Of course I didn't. I can't win!

I drop the kids back at my ex's. And she's all pissed at me for giving 'em Cracker Jacks for dinner. You know what? I love my kids. They want Cracker Jacks for dinner, they can have Cracker

Jacks for dinner. I was denied that love as a child when I was their age. And I'm not gonna do that to my own flesh and blood.

So she gets on the phone to her best friend complaining about how I'm not nurturing blah-blah-blah. Right in front of the kids. Emasculating me. Fortunately, I know what to do today. I calmly walked over to where she was standing, grabbed the phone, and pulled it off the wall. I did not throw it. I did not throw it.

And she goes berserk. Screaming and crying. Nuts. I'm like, "HEY GET OFF THE CROSS, WE NEED THE WOOD!" And I can't be around all that insanity today. It's too much for me.

But it's OK. You know, one thing I've learned here is that in every couple, there's two people. The lunatic and the sane one. And we know which one I am. I know when I'm not wanted, so I split.

So finally I get home. Fortunately Terry is there for me. Thank god for Terry, my only friend. She knows how to be there for me. She never takes my inventory, never judges me. Never yells at me. I mean, she barks at me every now and then when she wants to go out for a walk. But that's the thing about dogs. They're there for you. They're centered. I mean, Terry's got her shit figured out. I look into her eyes and she's so centered . . . "spiritual." Unqualified love. That's the only word for it.

Sometimes I think that's the only time I'm really at peace is when I'm sitting there with her watching TV. By the way, she loves all the same shows I do. It's like, "Why can't things always be like this?" You know? But I know why. Because the world is full of assholes, that's why.

And then *Oprah* comes on TV. She's got this guy, this doctor, and he says . . . right, shit! *(Checks watch)* OK, well, next Wednesday sounds good. Sure. And don't let me forget, I still owe you that seventy-five bucks from last month. You know, I really feel great coming here. I'm a completely different person now. I feel a breakthrough coming, don't you?

THE AUDITION

Walks over to "two people" and mimes shaking hands. His first handshake is warm and friendly, the second is respectful, slightly awed.

Oh, hey, how you doin'? You look great. Oh . . . Hi, hi, sir, it's an honor to meet you. Yeah.

(Steps back) Uh, just got back from L.A., actually. Pilot season, you know. *(Pause)* What was the last thing you would have seen me in? Uh, did you see *The Matrix*? I was in that, yeah. Did you see it? You know when Keanu was pushing through all those crowds of people on the sidewalk? I was one of those people on the sidewalk. Oh yeah, working with Keanu was great.

(Pulls pages of a script out of his back pocket.)

Yeah, she did . . . She said I should read pages twenty-five through thirty-five? Just twenty-five, OK. And my agent said it should be "intense but funny." *(Listens)* "Funny but intense." Right.

OK. *(Turns to an invisible video camera, starts to read from the script:)*

Hey, man, listen, it's not the end of the world. Linda isn't . . .

Wait, I'm sorry. Could I start again? I'm a little nervous.

(Settles, exhales, turns around, faces upstage, shakes hands out, returns:)

Hey man, listen, it's not the end of the world. Linda isn't the only woman in existence. Hey, I got an idea, my cousin Sharon is coming . . . uh . . .

(Changes inflection:)

Hey, I got an idea, my cousin Sharon is coming to town next week and why don't we all go out? Do something. *(Pause)* Of course she's good looking! Hey, man, would I lie about this to my own best buddy?

And listen, could I please also do page thirty-five? I worked pretty hard on it last night with my coach. Only take a sec . . .

Hey, man, listen, it's not the end of the world. I know, I know, I'd be pissed off, too . . . but how could I know she was a *lesbian*? *(Chuckles)*

What a great script. You know why this script is so great? It's *intelligent.*
So do you want me to try it a little more intense? A little funnier? It was perfect? Oh thanks, coming from you that means a lot to me.
So. OK! Uh, that's my new head shot. My new number is on the bottom. Or if you need to reach me this afternoon, I can give you my beeper number? You don't? Oh, OK. Well, I want to say thanks for, you know, asking me to come in. And I didn't want to say this before, but . . . uh, you're pretty much my favorite director. I see all your movies and I think you're a genius and really admire your work. *(Looks over at the "casting agent")* OK . . . I know, I've got to get going, too, we're all busy, OK . . . thanks . . . *(Again to the "director")*

Thank you. But before I go, could I ask you a question? I've been writing this screenplay and I was wondering if I wanted to get it to you, how would I do that? *(Again in response to the "casting agent")* OK, OK, heh, heh. Alright, I'll just drop it by the casting office. Yeah, I should go . . . but thank you again for having me . . . Right, I'll let you guys . . . I'm pretty busy, too . . . but thank you, thank you for having me . . . OK . . . 'Bye! *(Runs off)*

THE LADDER

Returns, calmly addresses the audience:

As embarrassing as all this looks, this is what's called "auditioning." In fact, that was a verbatim transcript of an audition I was on just last month. Actually, I'm exaggerating, I was much more obsequious.

It's important that I audition because it reminds me of why I became an actor in the first place. For the *pain*.

Because pain is important. Someday, when I'm riding around in my stretch limousine gazing out the tinted windows at all the losers out there living their humdrum existence, that pain will come in handy. I'll be able to say to myself: "I deserve this. I earned this. I PAID MY DUES, MAN."

Because that's what it's all about when you think about it, about making a supreme effort and rising up to another level of existence. Another plateau. Another *world* where everyone knows my name and wants my autograph and smiles at me wherever I go. Listens to my opinions even when I don't know what the hell I'm talking about. I'll go to a diner and the waitress will cut me an extra slice of pie. Go on a plane and the stewardess will flirt with me while she fluffs my pillow. I'll be walking down the street and someone will shout out the window: "HEY, ERIC! ALRIGHT, MAN!" And someone else will turn and say: "Is he somebody famous?" And a huge chorus will cry: "Don't you know who that *is?*"

I won't have to wait anymore. People will wait for *me*. No more lines at the bank, at the movie theatre. No more: *(Mimes secretary)* "Please hold, I'll see if he's in." No more: *(Mimes patronizing maître d')* "Yes, sir, we have your reservation right here. Your table will be ready in about forty-five minutes. Would you like to sit at the bar while you wait?" *(In response) No!* I don't want to sit at the bar. If I wanted to sit at a bar, I would have made a reservation at a bar, wouldn't I???

I'll be so rich and famous they'll throw people out of the restaurant just to make room for *me*! *(The patronizing maître d' rushes up to a table)* "I'm sorry, sir, someone more important than you has just arrived and we need the table. You have to go now. Please, hurry up. You can take your crème brûlée with you. You can eat it in the alley." *(Turns, his face lighting up)* "Yes, Mr. Bogosian, right this way, so happy you could join us this evening. We have a lovely table for you. Is this table to your liking?" *(Pulling out chair and fussing)* "Here's your napkin! Would you like ground pepper with that?" *(Realizing his mistake, he becomes completely flustered and backs away, twittering)* "Oh, Mr. Bogosian, Mr. Bogosian, Mr. Bogosian!!!" *(Bowing, scraping, licking the floor etc.)*

(Returns to normal voice, but more histrionic; addresses the audience:)

To be above the lines, above the crowds, above the norm! To be loved by millions never again to be touched by *one*! Never again to be crushed in the fray, everyone would know me, but from afar! Real far!

People will watch me on TV. I'll go on talk shows and everyone will be riveted as I go on and on about my dog's constipation. People want to know that stuff. I'll complain about how the power window in my stretch limo got stuck on the way to the show. *(Voice of guest on talk show)* "I just kept pushing the button and nothing happened, Dave! Just pushed the button, pushed the button." *(Normal voice)* The audience hanging on every word. *(Audience member in wide-eyed wonderment)* "You pushed the button, yes, and then?????"

(Normal voice) And Dave, good ol' Dave will clap and grin like an organ grinder's monkey, like I'm the smartest, funniest fuck he's ever met. And the audience will stand and cheer as I chatter on and on, because the tiniest moment in my life will be bigger than the biggest event in theirs.

See—there's another world and it's just like ours, but it's much much better. It floats above us. Call it heaven, call it Valhalla, call it Mount Olympus! Whatever you call it, the gods are there. I'm down here on earth, but I can see them up there. I can see the gods. They're having such a great time, And I want to be up there, too. Where every seat is first class. Where every room is a deluxe suite. Where the love of millions shines like a sun that never sets!

(Turns then looks back to the audience.)

Can you see them up there? Can you see the gods? Look at them. Aren't they beautiful? They're playing volley ball. There's Gwyneth passing off to Drew! Ooooh! Here comes Britney and she's just been cut off by Mariah! GO GIRL!!! Oh, and there's Michael Bolton getting down with Kenny G and, oh my goodness! Sting! They're gonna jam. And there's J. Lo and P. Diddy and LL and Eminem and all the other letters of the alphabet. And there's Madonna giving birth! How *intimate*! And Robin Williams is the attending physician. Marilyn Manson is the nurse! How cool is that?

My life is good, but the gods' life is better—better parties, better clothes, better cars, better sex, better breath. And see I'm going to get there some day, because I'm paying my dues. I can take the pain, I'm not afraid. My nose is too big, chop it off. My hair is too curly, straighten it. And what kind of name is "Eric Bogosian" anyway? It should be . . . "Ricky!" "Ricky Hanks." Much better name!

I'll make any sacrifice, do what it takes. You want me to play a serial killer who chops little children up and eats them for lunch? No problem-o. I'm an actor. Get humiliated by Tom Cruise? Where's the script? He wants to kick the piss out of me too? All the better, that's what I'm here for. *(Mimes getting ass kicked across the stage)* Oh, Tom, you're so intense! *(Crashes into the proscenium, revives, brushes himself off)* The location's six months in the deserts of Tierra del Fuego? Where's my plane ticket? Sure I have a wife, I have kids. I might not see them again for another five, ten, fifteen years. But when I'm rich and famous, they'll be happy I was gone all that time because they'll be rich and famous, too.

And sure, maybe I'll have to step on a few people as I make my way to the top. But every head I step on will be just another rung in the ladder of fame and fortune. Because I'm honest with myself. Let's face it, we're all on a ladder, from the lowliest beggar in Calcutta all the way up to Steven Spielberg, we all have our place. And it takes guts, it takes willpower and vision to reach up to that next rung and drag myself up. And sure when I get to the top, maybe all my friends will hate me but by then I'll have new friends. Better friends. *Everyone* will be my friend!

People will line up just to hang out with me, even my parents! They'll be like Mary and Joseph standing by the manger when all the kings came by. Puffed-up with pride like blowfish. And I'll be like baby Jesus, a godlet, on the straw for all to admire!

And when my new friends come by to visit, we'll be happy. We'll be happy together because now we can do what we've always wanted to do: just hang-out all day and think and talk about *ME*! Interviews with me! Photo calls with me! Me! Me! Me!

And when I get tired of my new friends, I'll say good night, climb into my king-sized four-poster bed, snuggle under the covers and pull out the remote control, and as my eyes slowly close, there I am again. On E! I'm on E! I'm on *Charlie Rose*. I'm on *Conan*! I'm on *Leno*! I'm a VH-1 veejay! I'm EVERYWHERE!

I'm *ubiquitous*! *(Becomes transformed, rising to his full height, arms out, emanating power)* God-like, like the sun, my rays shining down on every surface of the earth! My tentacles entwined around every mind, every imagination! *(Reprise of audience member on knees in awe)* "What is it like to be him?" *(Triumphant)* That's what they'll all want to know!

And *yes*, maybe some puny journalist will dare to question my talent. But I'll just say: "FUCK YOU! You're just a poor writer who lives in a tiny rental apartment who has to take the subway to work. I'm a big famous rich guy. I'll be around long after you're gone. Millions of people love me and no one gives a shit about you."

Even if I died tomorrow, it would make *headlines*. Because when the gods suffer, the world is *mesmerized*. Doesn't make any difference who they are: an ex-football-star crack-head wife-slaughterer; some reclusive high-pitched animal-loving child molester; a promiscuous "Adult Child of an Alcoholic" leader of the free world!

They're famous, they're in pain, we're *sad*.

Some little baby girl in a crib starves to death in the ghetto—no one cares. Why should they? She's a nobody. It's hard to work up an emotion over a "nobody."

(Drops into a chair, a guy at home watching TV, holding remote control, slightly animated:)

Hey, honey, look at this! Some little girl starved to death in her crib in the South Bronx! Terrible. How do those things happen? *(Pause, his face drops, ripples with emotion)* Oh, look, oh NO! Did you hear about *this*? *(Almost in tears, listening to the bad news)* Kelsey Grammer has a *urinary tract infection*! Oh shit! Wow. Oh, wait a minute . . . Shhhhh!!!

(Listens) It's OK, they're having a benefit! They're going to raise money to buy him a gold-plated catheter. Where's my checkbook? We gotta go to this thing. I don't want to miss it. I've always loved him.

(Stands, returns to normal voice, looks the audience straight in the eyes, god-like:)

Someday they'll say that about *me!*

IN THE AIR

Seated, addresses the audience.

I'm in the air now, moving from one place to the next. Everything is taken care of. I'm strapped in and I have a purpose
in life—arrive at LAX.

Things are good. My seat is comfy. I have a little white pillow and a little blue blanket. My John Grisham novel is compelling. And after dinner they'll be showing a movie, something with Tom Hanks in it. I like Tom Hanks because he's
happy. I'm happy that he's happy.

They even give us dinner. Not the kind of stuff I normally
eat, but they serve it so I eat it. An amazingly white roll with
butter, a salad and a salad dressing in a little plastic pouch,
made with guar gum. And for the main course I had, it was
good, I think it was either turkey or fish. And for dessert a little white rectangle with a red dot in the middle.

Now the stewardess comes by. She wants to know if I'm
OK, would I like anything to drink? Normally, no one cares
what I want, so this is very stimulating. Perhaps she really
does want to know. She's smiling at me. She's very pretty.
Maybe she likes me. Maybe she's flirting with me? I know
what this is about. I know how to do this.

*(Transforms from mild-mannered speaker to self-assured
passenger, addressing the stewardess, acting as if he could
care less:)*

I'll have a Diet Coke, no ice. And I'll keep the can. Thanks. *(Takes can, checks his watch)* Say do you know if the flight is on time? Cool. Wow. You must fly this flight all the time, huh? Just back and forth. What is that accent? Ohio? Really, where? Columbus? Yeah, that's a great town. Little movie theatre downtown. So I'm curious, you fly into L.A. . . . *(Takes his drink)* Oh, thanks . . . And then just turn around and dead-head it back to New York? Oh, you stay overnight in Los Angeles? That sounds like fun. It isn't? It sucks? Yeah, I heard that airport hotel is pretty bad. *(Answering)* Four Seasons, it's very comfortable. *(Getting more and more casual)* You know it's funny that you should say you find L.A. boring. Do you know who Ricky Martin is? Well, his business manager's brother-in-law is good friends with my brother-in-law and he's got this sold-out concert tonight at the Hollywood Bowl . . . oh, so you know about it, yeah, well anyway, they laid like two free tickets on me, front row center, and I don't really know anybody in L.A. to take. You know what? I've never done anything like this before, forget it. *(Mock surprise)* You would? Well, you'd really be doing me a favor. Yeah, yeah, well check, make your call. You know where to find me. OK. 'Bye. *(Breathy)* See you in a while.

(Aside to the audience:)

I can see she's thinking about the free tickets to the Ricky Martin concert. If only she knew what I was thinking. I've been checking out her butt every time she turned around for the last hour and a half. Nice butt. Nice tight Columbus, Ohio, butt.

Yeah, we'll go to that Ricky Martin concert and then we'll go out to some trendy L.A. nightspot that only cool people like me know about. But we'll be above it all and leave once we get past the velvet ropes. And then . . . then we'll go for a ride . . . but they roll up the sidewalks at ten P.M. in L.A., so we'll have to go back to my room at the Four Seasons. And she'll be impressed by the four-star-edness of the whole thing—the cashews in the little mason jar, the free playing cards. We'll sit on the couch and talk about life for about three minutes, then we'll start kissing, tear each other's clothes off.

And I'll get that tight little United Airlines outfit off and that Wonderbra and that thong she doesn't think I notice underneath. And she'll be completely NUDE. Just like Mary Elizabeth when we were six playing doctor behind the elementary school. I'll be able to examine her all I want: toes, knees, belly button.

And then I'll say, "Why don't we take a shower?" That's always a good icebreaker. Girls like that. And we'll kiss under the flowing water, very erotic. And then I'll say, "Why don't I wash your back?" And I'll lather her up. I'll cover her with lather, I won't stop at her back. She'll be all white from all the lather and I won't wash her off . . . I'll just *(Mimes picking her up and carrying her)* carry her to the bed and she'll be this big slick white lathered-up stewardess. And I'll spread her legs and the only thing I'll be able to see through all the soap bubbles is a little pink sideways smile looking up at me. And I'll lean over, and with my tongue I'll very very gently place the tip of my tongue . . .

(Jumps behind the mike; deep, resonant, good-ol'-boy captain's voice:)

This is your captain speaking. We're currently cruising at an altitude of about thirty thousand feet with clear skies all the way in to LAX, making up a little time for that delayed departure. Which is the good news. *Bad* news is we got a little problem up here in the cockpit. Nothing to get too concerned about. Seems that when we were refueling back at JFK, the fuel gauge got stuck and thing is, we're not carrying a whole helluvalot of fuel this afternoon. In fact, we're pretty much bone dry.

Now you're probably asking yourself, What does that mean to me? Well, it means we're going to have to try a little landing here this afternoon. And as I just said, we are currently thirty thousand feet over the Colorado Rockies. Beautiful time of year. If you look out the right side of the cabin you can see the aspens just turning golden there on the mountainsides. Those of you who are skiers are probably familiar with Vail or Beaver Creek. Me and the wife have a little timeshare down around Eagle. We go down there for about three weeks every winter. Not that I'm much of a skier myself, I prefer those bass-fishing shows on cable TV. But I digress. We're going to be attempting a forty-five degree descent this afternoon. So please check that your seatbelts are fastened securely about your middle with your tray tables in their upright and locked position, and no moving about the cabin, please, as we make our descent. Now when we land, or I should say "scrape" into a landing, it's gonna feel kinda bumpy, kinda like we're crashing, but let me assure all of you on-board today that in the rare event we actually do crash, you . . . you won't feel a thing. You'll be knocked unconscious instantly, they'll be lucky if they can find our teeth when this is all over. So I'm gonna sign off now, try and concentrate on what I'm doing, instead of sounding like a damn jackass with one foot in the grave, let you get back to that movie you're watching. What is it, Billy? *Forrest Gump?* Love that flick: "You never know what you're going to get"! *(Puts his hand over the mike)* Billy, is the black box turned on? Give it a good thump with your fist. Thanks, bro. *(Full voice)* And let me remind all of you on-board this afternoon, we at United know you have a choice of airlines when you fly and we appreciate your patronage. Have a nice day.

THE CRASH

Jumps in front of the mike, addresses the audience breathlessly while miming prayer:

And everyone on the plane has suddenly become deeply religious, praying silently, each and every one of them to his or her own secret, benevolent and all-powerful god that he doesn't let the giant tin monster go swimming into some whacky air current and drag them sideways into the mountainside like one gigantic scraping aluminum fireball millions of other middle-class Americans can watch on the evening news.

(Switches gears, surfer voice, another guy watching TV, holding a remote control:)

Oh wow, Heather, you should see this! No, it's not the new Limp Bizkit video, it's CNN, I turned it on by mistake. Whoa! A plane crashed in Colorado and they're showing it live. Wow! *(Pause)* 767! Rammed right into the health club at the Hyatt in Beaver Creek. Wow. Bodies all over the snow! Imagine what that must be like to be in that plane just before you hit. Like you know you're going to be completely flattened in about thirty seconds. Like you won't exist anymore. Every thought you ever had will disappear. All those phone numbers!

Or imagine you're in the health club working on your pecs, looking out the plate-glass window checking out the mountains and *(Sees the plane coming right at him)* . . . and you're like, "Oh shit," but you don't even have time to say, "shit," *(Mimes being blown backward)* and then you're covered with aviation fuel and you're jumping around frying alive in the snow . . . oh, Heather, that reminds me did you order the crispy duck from Hunan Palace yet? I want my sauce on the side!

(Reverts to normal voice, speaks directly to audience:)

But of course, if that actually happened . . . But then I'll be immortal. Which is what I've always wanted. I'll be up there with the gods. Nothing like a plane crash to confer immortality. Way better than a drug overdose. And you'd be happy because you would have seen one of my last performances. It would be historic. Historic and ironic. *(Audience member)* "Yeah, it was incredible: he kept talking about plane crashes and then he was *in* a plane crash!" *(Pause)* "Really makes you think!"

But then I'll be dead, which would be bad for me. No fun at all. *(Inspiration strikes)* I know, I'll *survive*. I'll be a survivor and I'll sell my story! Everyone will want to take a meeting with me. I will finally have arrived in L.A. *(Snaps fingers)*

THE MEETING

With great effort, he drags the chair to center stage. His nasal voice is aging but energetic:

Eric, come on in. Siddown. Siddown. *(Points to chair)* So happy you could take the time from your busy schedule to come by. Siddown, siddown. You want anything to drink? We got it all, espresso, soy milk, guava juice, water from a melted glacier, whatever you need. Hold on a second. *(Calling off)* NAOMI! Would you come in here for a moment please? You met Naomi on your way in. She's your biggest fan, has pictures of the plane crash tacked up all over her desk *(Introducing them to each other)* This is Naomi, my brilliant assistant. What would you like, Eric? Just coffee? How do you take that? With milk? *(Walks around the chair, gestures toward Naomi, as if she's standing before them)* You know, Eric, Naomi just graduated from the film school at Columbia University. Studied with *Milos Foreman.* How about that? She's writing a screenplay about the history of *feminism.* Isn't that something? *(Gazes at "Naomi" with admiration; then abruptly)* *Coffee.* With milk. Thank you. *(Following her out; brusque)* And, Naomi, did you call the guy at Range Rover? Did they get the stain off the seat? Follow up on that, please, Naomi. I got that Richard Gere benefit for the Dalai Lama tonight. *(Returning to "Eric")* I can't show up at a Buddhist benefit in a dirty Range Rover, now can I?

A beautiful girl isn't she? Not that I'm about to make a move. Not these days. Not these days. You know, Eric, in the old days everything was different. We were changing the world and we were having a great time doing it. Made movies about important stuff, we shook people up. Blew people's minds and then we got blown. Now everything's about money. Where's the fun anymore? What happened to the revolution? What's wrong with a couple of lines, a little reefer, some free love? No, go to rehab, go directly to rehab, do not pass go, do not collect two hundred thousand dollars! No more fooling around for me. All I do now is lie on the couch like an old dog and lick my balls.

(Mimes grabbing a handful of something.)

You smoke cigars, Eric? Here, take one of these. I have a guy sends 'em up to me from Honduras. They're so hard to roll, the peasants go blind making 'em. Enjoy.

But Eric, I want to tell you, we all watched it on the news, and it was so dramatic! We were riveted. The burning plane, the ambulances, the helicopters, the bodies in the snow. It was almost dramatic. And I turned to my wife and I said, "Michelle, I have to make this movie." You understand? For me, for me. Not for the money. I don't need the money. I have all the money I need. I could have you killed right now if I wanted to, that's how much money I have.

For the humanitarian message, Eric. I want to get your story out there, Eric, because people have to hear it. Because people need a positive message in their lives, Eric.

They're tired of the negative stuff. Nobody ever changed the world with negativity, Eric. They know the world is fucked-up—the ozone layer is kaput, there are terrorists around every corner, poor people in every nook and cranny—who the fuck wants to hear all that negative shit? Me, I don't even watch the news anymore. Sarajevo one year, Bosnia the next, Kosovo the next. Wrap it up already. Move on!

People don't want negativity, they want to be inspired, they want hope. They need your story. You know why? The audiences today, their lives suck. They're holding down two jobs, their kids are all on drugs, all they have to look forward to is a slow death by cancer. If it weren't for the inspiration they get from movies and TV, they'd jump off a cliff like a bunch of lemmings.

And that's what you gave 'em when they thought everyone on that plane was dead and you came walking out of the wreckage. Tears came to my eyes, I was so moved.

(Looks up suddenly) What? Naomi, bring it in. Don't just stand there. Bring it in and put it on the table! Did you bring him a napkin? Don't I always tell you, bring a napkin. Naomi, listen to me, NAP-KIN, N-A-P-K-E-N. Just put it down. It's OK, it's OK, get out.

It's mythic. Like something out of the Greek myths. Like the Phoenix rising out of the ashes. You know what the Phoenix was, Eric? It rose out of the ashes. And that's you! They thought everyone was dead, and out you came out of the burning wreck . . . with that stewardess in your arms. And then you gave her mouth-to-mouth resuscitation right there on the snow in front of fifty million people. That was incredible.

You survived. You saved that stewardess and you fell in love. I hear you're living together now. Getting married. What a heartwarming story. I mean, I'm very sorry about your divorce, how long were you married? Nineteen years. It happens, it happens. Kids? Yeah, that's always tough . . . but you know, they learn from it, Eric. It's good for them. That's what we're here for, to teach our kids. *Kids.* Mine are all grown. The oldest is just going through her own divorce, the middle one just got out of rehab, the baby's not even speaking to me.

But you know what I say to those kids? *(Flips him the bird)* Fuck you! Because that's not what's important for people like us, Eric. Artists like you and me. Our work, our humanitarian message is what's important. The positive message we have to send, that's what it's all about. The humanitarian message of love.

SHEEP

Yeah, yeah, yeah, yeah, yeah, yeah. I'm so smart.

(Interrupts himself, picks up chair and almost hurls it, sets it down again and begins pacing the stage.)

In my black jeans and my righteous anger, ranting on and on about hypocrisy, pissing people off just enough to sell a few tickets. Always looking over my shoulder, making sure I don't lose my place in the big line. Desperately trying to preserve my modicum of success so that I can hold my head high in this giant pecking order of art and commerce and first-class plane tickets.

I'm a bullshit-slinger. That's all I am. One more bullshit-slinger from a long tradition of bullshit-slingers. A hypocrite. What do I do that's so *courageous* or *selfless* that gives me the right to say shit about shit?

And you, you come in here and get all fluffed up and expectant like a bunch of baby birds with your beaks wide open, waiting to be fed. But I've got bad news for you. I'm all out of worms today. Sorry! I'm empty. I'm a vacuum. I'm a black hole.

I'm just a mirror. I'm up here thinking about what you're thinking about what I'm thinking. Even right now, while I'm saying all this I'm hoping, They'll think this is really pushing it! *(Audience member)* "My God! Now he's gone too far!" But I haven't gone *anywhere*. I'm still here. And so are you. We're all here. We haven't moved an inch.

I'm just some skinny guy with curly hair and black jeans. My distinguishing characteristic is the brand of bottled water I drink. Which HBO TV show I prefer.

The big choices in my life are between the *Star Wars* prequel or the *Austin Powers* sequel. The Big Mac or the Grilled Chicken. *(Scratches his chin, pondering)* "Tall" or "grandé." Yeah, those are the big decisions in *my* life.

I'm not fighting the system, I'm *part* of the system. *I toe the line.* And I do it for a very good reason: I'm a sheep. I am a gutless sheep.

So when they say, "Get in line," I get in line, you know? It isn't like I *want* to be in line. I *hate* getting in line. "I'm a rebel, man! I used to smoke pot! I marched in Washington against something once. I love to drive around in my four-wheel drive, blasting Rage Against the Machine with my seat-belt cinched tightly around my flabby middle! That's the kind of rebel I am.

Yeah, I'm a rebel, alright, but in the long run I have to get in line. I better fucking get in line. That's the deal. Because if I don't, then maybe nobody will, and if nobody gets in line, then what do you have? Chaos!

And if things get really chaotic, what's going to happen to *me*? I'm going to *lose*. Because I mean that's the whole point of civilization isn't it? To protect the weak against the strong! And when things get out of control, it's the bad guys who take over. And I'm no bad guy, I'm no Hun! I'm no Mongol! I'm no bad-ass. I'm no Hell's Angel.

(Jumps into gruff biker voice:)

You know when you just had sex . . . You're lying on the bed, the two of yas, you're all spaced-out. All sweaty and smelly, you smell like a couple of camels at the zoo. You got stuff all stuck all over ya. Your hair's all pushed over to one side. She's lying there, she's got a big puddle of come on her belly.

And you're like writing your name in the come on her belly. Then you go south. And then you start fooling with her honey pot. Stirring the honey, oh yeah.

And she's like, "OHHHHHH!" And then she reaches over and starts yanking on your joystick and the two of you are like, "OOOOOHHHH!! AAAHHHHHH!" Next thing you know: Oh, look who's back in action, the little soldier! He's ready for another battle!

So you get ready to do it again, because the second time's always the best, you know what I mean? Always more intense. And you get ready to stick it in . . . But what do you gotta do before you stick the little doggy in the doghouse? What do you always haveta do? Get out the hash pipe, right?

One hit on the hash pipe. Toss some coke on her tits, lick it up. And then you slide it in nice and slow. You stick her toes in your ears, she sticks her thumb up your asshole. You grab her ass, she grabs your butt. She's screaming, you're barking . . . *(Thrusting and shouting)* "OH, OH, OH, OH, OH!" BOOOOOOM—and you come so hard you feel like you're gonna be brain-damaged for the rest of your life, and you fall back onto the bed, but just before your head hits the pillow you grab that bottle of tequila, take one last hit as your brain does a slow dive into a deep black hole of complete and utter *satisfaction*.

(Normal voice:)

Yeah, I can talk the talk, but I can't walk the walk.

I'm weak and I'm scared. So I get in line. Like a sheep. Like a *cow*. So I stand in line like everybody else. Patiently waiting my turn to get to the head of the line so I can get conked on the head, a chain wrapped around my legs, get pulled upside-down to have my throat slit. My blood drained and ground into hamburger. That's the kind of rebel *I* am.

Just show me the line and I'll get in it. I need the line. The line is my friend.

And when the bad guys in the steel-tipped boots do show up and kick down my door in the middle of the night, I won't be a hero. No. I'll say, "I've completely re-thought the revolution." *(Runs and hides behind the chair)* And I'll cower under my bed. I'll say, "I don't want to bother anybody, in fact I don't have any opinion about anything actually. I was just pretending to be a rebel. I'm just a little dog, see?" *(Barks a short, timid bark, gets up and starts running in large circles)* Like a little dog. Like a little dog. I just want to be safe. I just want to hang out with all the other little dogs and run around and chase cars and sniff other doggies' butts and piss on trees. Just give me a bowl of water and pat my head and tell me I wrote a nice screenplay and I'll wag my tail and go sleep on the couch and not bother anybody.

(Curls up on chair.)

I just want to be one of the pack, an ingredient, a component, a cog on the wheel. That's what I am, a cog! A cog dog. *(Stands on the chair)* Cog dog, cog dog, cog dog, cog.

(Barks three long howls.)

THE HIGHWAY

Effects of cars passing. Lights up reveal man standing with his thumb out, hitching. Stoner voice:

I hope we get a ride pretty soon, man, it's getting cold out here. *(Puts his hand up in refusal)* No coffee for me, man, it's not my thing anymore. You know? All those little starving peasant coffee farmers down in South America? I don't want to be responsible for all that, you know? Like you're either part of the problem or you're part of the solution. No coffee, no sugar, no meat, no Nikes. It's all connected man, it's all part of the big picture. If you don't believe that, then it's like we're living in a giant TV screen that isn't tuned to any station. Billions of dots, bouncing and frying around. Noise in a void. Snow. Dots. But there's always a big picture. Sometimes you can't see it, but it's there.

(Effect of car passing.)

Last night I was hitching, and for a few minutes everything made sense. The stars were floatin' high in the sky. I could smell the grass. The crickets were cricketing. I was in harmony with the universe.

And then I heard this sound from far away: BEP. BEP. And then I saw it, this giant eighteen-wheeler blowin' down on me, doing ninety miles an hour. And I looked up through the windshield, I could see the driver. One of those bizarro zombies from our modern-day life. Big thick neck. Beard stubble. Circles under his eyes from all the porno videos he's been watchin'. Totally *insane!* Chowin' on this huge meatball sub as he drove.

And I thought, That pretty much sums it up. Meatballs, man. Like what's the karma in a meatball? Only humans make balls out of other animals. Like when you're in kindergarten and you're coloring in your coloring book: what does the doggy say? "Bow-wow!" What does the kitty say? "Mee-oww." What does the moo-cow say? "AARRGGGHHHHHH!!!!!!"

Oh yeah, dude tried to run me over, man! And as I jumped out of the way and he blew past, he had his window down and he was swearing at me. "FUCK YOU, YOU LOSER SHIT FREAK FUCKIN' PIECE OF SHIT ASSHOLE SUCK MY DICK YOU FUCKHEAD FUCK FUCK FUCK!"

Spitting out these gobs of phlegm because he's filled with mucus from all the dairy products he consumes! And then reached up and . . . BLAAAAAP! BLAAAAAP! BLAAAAAP!

Totally fucked me up, man. Couldn't hear the crickets for hours. Like what's an airhorn, man, but the sound of the end of civilization?

See I can't be around all that toxic shit anymore, man. Cannot do it. That's why I hit the road, man. Oh yeah, I just went into the boss one day and said, "I'm outta here." What? Oh, he didn't care, he's got people lined up around the block to make those lattes. He just looked at me and said, "What are you going to do for money?"

And I said, "I don't need money, man. Money's just to buy stuff. And I don't need stuff. I'm free. I mean, look around us, man, all these cars, always movin' out on the highway. They never stop. Like ants in an anthill. Ever watch ants, man? I love watchin' ants, man. Always busy doing something really important like moving a cookie crumb from here *(Indicates)* all the way over to there. That's what all these cars are doin', just movin' stuff around. But instead of popsicle sticks and bits of chewed-up leaf, they're movin' DVDs and running shoes and frozen turkey burgers and microwave popcorn and flawless pieces of fruit with the little stickers on 'em that you can't get off . . . back to the anthill.

Oh, my boss? He said, "Yeah, well you'll be singing another song when you're old."

And I said, "When I'm old same thing'll happen to me that's going to happen to you. I'm gonna die. Except that *you're* gonna be so rich with your portfolios and mutual funds and IRAs and all that shit they won't *let* you die. They'll stick you in one of those old-age cells with adjustable beds that go up and down and a remote control for a TV set. Just hope you're not paralyzed or you'll be watchin' Home Shopping Network 'round the clock for the rest of your feeble life.

Me, when I die, I'm just gonna curl up on a pile of leaves in the middle of the woods and croak. And maybe if I'm lucky, an acorn will get lodged in my butt crack. And a giant oak tree will grow out of my ass and drop acorns all over my grave. And then a deer will come and munch on those acorns and my karma will go from those acorns into that deer. And then a mountain lion will come and eat the deer and my karma will go into that lion sperm and when the lion makes it with his old lady I'll come back as a baby lion. *(Mimes the baby mountain lion padding about)* Spend my next life in the woods, just boppin' around doin' that mountain lion thing.

Oh, he just gave this weird look, patted me on the back and said, "Good luck, dude."

And I said, "I don't need the luck, man, you're the one on the Titanic."

Alaska. Just gonna take this highway as far as it goes, then find a road and take it as far as it goes, then find a path and walk it until there's no more path, until I'm completely surrounded by woods. And then I'm gonna step right into the wilderness. Just live on berries and shit. Not bother anybody. Not hurt anything.

Something I have to do, man. Because I'm a first-class passenger on the spaceship Earth. I've got a one-way ticket so I have to make the ride count, you know? And as far as I figure it, you can either take the service road or the scenic route. And, man, if I only have one ride, I want it to be beautiful.

And if nobody ever hears from me again, you know, it'll be OK. If nobody knows where I am, I won't mind, because I'll know where I am, and that's the most important thing.

(Jumps back as three cars pass in succession, followed by an enormous truck. He watches in stunned dismay as it passes, roaring into the night.

Fade to black.)

ORPHANS

When I put a solo together, I assemble it like a jigsaw puzzle. Some monologues don't fit, but I like them too much to throw them away. I call them "Orphans." Sometimes they've been performed only one or two times, sometimes never. Sometimes they contain lines or ideas that become part of other monologues.

REACH OUT

Guy briskly takes a seat for an interview. He takes a sip from a cup of coffee every now and then.

Hey, hey! Hi! Nice to be meet you, thanks, man. Yeah, sure, a lot going on. The festival. The awards. Then, you know, number one at the box office. It's cool. Sure. Sure. Wow. Very exciting, you know. I feel like a big deal.

Well, we fought hard to get this movie made, because it was something we believe in. The corporate suits at the big studios basically said this was a movie that could never be made and, you know, nobody wanted to see a movie like this and, we, uh, proved them wrong so, uh, you know, it's nice to have them kissing our ass now, so to speak. Hah. Hah. Not that I'm bitter or anything.

And I don't want to take all the credit. Without Harry Horntoad at Seminal Films believing in us, it never would have been made. He believed in the cause, and he believed we could really reach a lot of people. And we did. You know, like they say, if a tree falls in a forest and nobody hears it fall, does it make a sound?

Well, maybe I'm getting a big head about myself here, but I think, maybe, *maybe* I changed things for the better just a little bit, just one little bit. If *one* homeless person can sleep indoors tonight because of what I've done, then I've done my job. I can say: "I told America—you have a homeless problem." And I did. And you know a portion of the receipts from the picture go directly to homeless relief. Which is cool. You know?

Well, I did move out of my old place, I lived on Sunset for ten years and as exciting as I find street junkies and male hookers to be, it was time to move on.

Last week? Last week, seven million. So far, we've grossed sixty-seven million, four hundred and thirty-five thousand. But who's counting, right?

No I don't have five Porsches!!! Shit, where does the media get this stuff? *Three* Porsches, man. But you know man, I've always liked Porsches. They were just something I've always wanted. And it's like, why not? You know?

Yes, I did just sign a new deal with Seminal for two million a picture, but you have to understand that they won't pay me the money if I don't *make* them the money. I mean that's what it's all about. And the thing is that I really want to make movies that make money and I want to reach people.

I really want to get my message across . . . Hmmmm? Well, it's just that we should all love one another and hope for a better world, and, um, that, uh, if we all work together and stop all this hate . . . I mean, I don't want to be radical about any of this. I think that people who take a radical point of view really cut themselves off from everybody else. I don't want to do that. I was at a show just a few days ago in New York, this Armenian comedian was at this place on the Lower East Side. Interesting stuff, the guy's talented. But *nasty*, you know? Like negative. And how many people come to his show? A hundred? No one hears his message. Millions of people hear my message, man.

The next movie? Well, talking with the executives at the studio, we felt that it would be good for me to sort of explore another subject the way we did the homeless. I mean, Gary was so great as Chuck, the homeless guy in my movie, we wanted to do something else with Gary. And so what he's doing in my next picture is he will be playing a retarded drug addict. I should say a "mentally handicapped" drug addict. Because I think, you know, uh, drugs are terrible. And I think, it's also pretty terrible to be, you know, retarded. And Gary's such a great actor. The next De Niro. He's been hanging out with retarded people, talking to them and stuff. You should have seen him on the show. He's so fucking funny—oops!

Oh, OK. Yeah. Well, thank you. You really liked it? You did? Well, thanks. Thanks, man. It means a lot to me. It means a lot to me because I know you really care, and I care, and I care that you care.

Thank you. I hope so. Well come on up to the new place next weekend and I'll give you a ride in one of my Porsches. Thanks. Thanks a lot, g'night.

NO CRIME

Walking around an empty chair, extra large Starbucks coffee cup in his hand. Excited, talks to the chair in a hip-hop voice:

Yo dude, check it out. Guy getting handcuffed on TV. Dig it. I love this show, man—watch, watch they're going to search his vehicle, man! Looking for the ganja. Yeah, yeah, they found it. Oh, oh, time to go to jail, my friend. Uh-huh. You made a big fucking mistake, big fucking mistake, you got *caught.*

Like, I'm in the supermarket yesterday and they've got this new thing, they give you a little card. And this card has all your personal shit on it and then every time you use the card, a data bank collects all the information about you. Like, yo: "Drinks Diet Coke, buys lots of Advil, doesn't eat meat." Like an alarm goes off somewhere if you DEVIATE.

'Cause that's the deal, man: they're looking for the dangerous deviates. That's why I made myself invisible, dude. They're not going to find me. No license, no credit cards, no shit. They want everybody to have an identity card. They puttin' those satellite locator chips in the cell phones. Oh yeah, that would make things easy when they start arresting everybody.

No crime. Gonna live in a no-crime world. Like the chickens they keep in those little cages with the food tray rolling by them. Happy fucking chickens. Cluck-cluck-cluck! Awwwkkkk!

It's just ant sugar, man. Just like bits of sugar they give us to trick us to eat the poison. The machine, man, knows what we want, better than we do. Sugar, fat, drugs, porno videos, popcorn in the microwave, Prozac and *People* magazine. DVDs, SUVs, MP3s, XTC. It feeds us and we like leeches. Suck. Suck. Like velcro, the system is the hooks and we the loops.

Yo, yo, yo, yo, yo . . . check it out. Guy's walking his dog. See, he walks the dog, but all the time, the dog thinks he's walking the man . . . Are we walking the computers or they walking us?

Check it out. Like the "revolution." Wow, man. "I am ANTI the establishment. I am alternative." Uh-huh. I'm into SONGS about guns and sex. Shit.

I remember the first time I got a tattoo, man. I was *expressing* myself. Just like those models in the ads, man. All those junkies in *Vogue* magazine.

Like I went into a bookstore and I bought a book. Was about revolution, real revolution. And what they do during a real revolution is, they kill people. Lots of people. That's history, man.

Human beings, they be killing each other and they make piles of stuff. Trash. Possessions. Bodies. No other animal makes piles. Or kills itself.

The way we do, man. You know who Tamerlane was, man? He killed some folks. Made piles out of their *skulls*. Torquemada. Hannibal. Stalin. Hitler. All the great people in history that we remember killed shitloads of other people, threw 'em in piles. Lincoln, man, Abraham Lincoln. People died on his watch, big time.

I used to sky dive. I used to see how far I could fall before pulling the cord. I'd look down at all the people and they were just like little ants. All these little ants whizzing as fast as they can in their carcinogenic gas-powered go-carts.

The system looks down at us from far above.

(Upper-crust voice:)

Look at the little ants, the foolish little ants, working all day and night. We will have them hurry and scurry for us, because they have no brain, they are only ants. We will convince them that they have caused their own unhappiness, that if only they had more discipline, they would be happy. Fools! Hah-hah! Let's sell them some more self-help books!

(Back to hip-hop voice:)

See, a few years ago, I'd be hanging out with my friends. And it would be like, "What's on TV?" Nothing. "What's in the movies?" Nothing. "Wanna eat some shit?" No. "Wanna smoke a dube?" No. Nothing, man. It got so there was nothing. Heroin. Nothing. Pierce my dick. Nothing. Then what? After nothing?

You say OK, here it comes another day in my life. Let's see here, a little sex, a little exercise, a few cigarettes, maybe a frappuccino . . . now what? You know? NOW WHAT THE FUCK HAPPENS??

One time I was diving the sky over this shopping mall. And I thought, I just won't pull the cord. All these folks will be shopping and shit and—BOOM—I'll come through the ceiling right on their fat suburban asses.

But I didn't do it. I could have, but I didn't. 'Cause I'd realized while I was falling in the air down to the shopping center, What difference does it make? You know? I mean if I had been a Nazi at the Siege of Stalingrad I'd be just a frozen corpse chewing on some icy dirt. But if I were Barbra Streisand I'd be in a hot tub watching the sun set.

So I think, OK, get a gun. Blow some minds. I mean even Ed Gein was happy they put him in jail. It's like OK, it's just one more thing. They got TV in jail too, you dig.

Otherwise, it's just playing into the hands of the comput-ers. Every year goes by, the computers think faster, figure out human desire better. We're running around watching videos, climbing all over each other like crabs in a bottle, while our sperm count goes down, down, down.

It's like this, something rocks the boat, make it a sin. The worse the sin, the better it feels. But don't do it. No fucking around. No taking drugs. No stealing. But all that shit's the stuff the big cats do all the time. *All* the time. They do everything bad. That's why they want to be big rich motherfuckers in the first place, so they can do the bad shit. Then one day, when they seventy-five years old, they wake up in the middle of the night and go, "Oh shit, I've been an *asshole* all this time. Sorry."

So I say, put a bullet in the chamber, lock and load, motherfucker. You know? You know what I'm saying? Do you? Draw a line in the sand . . . pick a victim, it really don't make no diff who. Let's face it, just a bunch of ants. You ever step on ants? Sure you did.

VICTIM

Limping. Shaking a cigarette out of a pack.

Just hold your horses here alright? I'll tell you in a second,
Terry. Wait a minute, my leg, my leg. *(Hobbles, fumbles with
cigarette)* Hold on, hold on, let me light my cigarette here.
I'll tell ya, just shut up. Alright? So I . . . so what happened
was, wait a minute *(Takes forever to light his cigarette)* so
I goes down to welfare, right? And I gets my check. And
I pick up my methadone, right? So I say to myself I'll snag a
carton of Benson & Hedges, go home, drink my zombie juice,
space, order up some chicken wings and shrimp fried rice—
you know how I love my shrimp fried rice? Maybe take a
bath, watch a little *Oprah* with Snowball. I deserve it.
I deserve it. Been very stressed lately. What with Sondra calling me night and day. Oh yeah, she calls. She calls. Always
bitchin' about the kid. You know he's in college now. Oh
yeah. And she calls me wantin' money, you know? And I say
to her, Sondra, if I had the money I'd send the money. I love
my kid, you know? I DON'T HAVE ANY FUCKING
MONEY! Wait a sec, I'll get to the leg, I'll get to the leg!

So I gets home, I'm waitin' for the Chink food to get deliv-
ered and I'm taking a minute to catch my breath, got Snowball on my lap and for two seconds—I'm happy. The phone
rings. It's Sondra. Like she's got radar: "He's happy, I better
call him and give him shit." And she starts with the money.
And what can I say? I wish I had the money. I play Lotto
every fucking day hoping I could get some money together to

send to my kid. But the odds, Terry, the odds are stacked against me, always have been. So I hangs up on her and pull the phone outta the wall. That does it. Fuck the food. I'm doin' the methadone now. So I gets out the bottle and all of a sudden there's a knock on the door. Who is it? Carol, that satanic bitch. She just copped, she's lookin' for a place to fix, right? So she's gonna lay twenty bucks on me so she can sit on my couch and catch a nod, right? So I'm sittin' there, trying to stay calm, watchin' her tryin' to hit a vein, gettin' blood all over the place. Finally I say, "Here let me do that," and I find a spot in her neck, she got a great neck, hit her good. She's out so fast, I'm bootin' her 'cause you know if I take the spike out, she's gonna be pissed. Right?

And I'm gone to the races, Terry. What else could I do? I can taste the junk in the roof of my mouth. I mean I'm scopin' how she's nodding her face off like a wax dummy on a hot day, the cigarette burning her fingers, the needle in her neck. It's pushin' all my buttons, you know? I'm thinkin', That would feel real good right now, after all I been through. Very refreshing.

So I say, "Wake up, Carol, you win, forget it with the twenty bucks, just lay a bag on me."

Just then the Chink food shows up and the guy, you know the way those guys are, kinda lookin' at you like they don't know what you're saying, and I'm just like cool, cool, here's the money for the food, get lost, you know? I had no appetite. Guy's standin' in the door, Snowball's barkin' at 'im, she hates the Chinese people, don't ask me why. Carol's cleaning drops of blood off those black leather pants a hers she's so proud of. I'm thinkin', People are fuckin' weird, ya know?

Anyway, I finally gets rid of the Coolie, I stick the wings and the fried rice in the fridge so the roaches can't get at it, although I once found a roach in an ice cube, don't ask me how that got there. And Carol says, "I don't got no more. We gotta go cop."

And you know how it is, Terry, when that monkey wakes up. He doesn't just wake up, he takes speed. Hoppin' up and down on my back like he's on a two-hundred-pound pogo stick. So I say, fine, let's take a walk. So I had this C-note stashed away—I know I owe you money, Terry, I know, but hey, man, will you be decent for once in your skinny-assed, cheapskate life? I don't even know why I bother talkin' to you. You know? Do you want to hear the story or not? Alright, so where was I?

We go cop. And we get beat. You know how it is, whenever you're desperate, you get beat. It's like life, man. It's like fuckin' life. So that's a hundred bucks down the drain. Then I remember, I didn't do the methadone yet. So me and Carol hikes back to my place, I walks in the door, Snowball is completely confused, we grab the 'done and go back to the corner where my usual guy is, and we sell the shit and I buy four bags.

And we come back to my place and she says, "You owe me two bags." And I say, "Why?" And she says, "'Cause I took you to my cop spot." And I said, "I got beat at your cop spot, you bitch." And she starts yelling at me and shit, but, man, fuck me if I'm going to lay two bags on her for gettin' ripped off. Plus, she never paid me for hanging in the first place.

Suddenly she gets real sweet on me and says, "OK, just gimme one." So I do. And then I bang a bag and it's not as good as what she had, but it's OK on account that my dealer knows I'm trying to get straight so he wants me to have a good taste. OK. No. There's none left. 'Cause I closed my eyes for two seconds, next thing I know, Carol's gone, my dope's gone, the front door's open and Snowball's out on the landing barking her furry brains out.

So I'm kinda high but I'm also pissed off, so I jump up and run to the door to get the dog back inside before she gets kidnapped or some shit like that, but I'm running so hard that when I run out my door, I keeps going and I goes right off the landing—CRASH-BOOM—down the stairs all the way down by where the mailboxes are.

And Snowball's standing at the top of the stairs kinda lookin' at me, she's not barkin' anymore she's just giving me this look like, Why'd you do that? Right? And I try to move but I can't so I figure something must be broken. And the assholes who live in my building are coming into the building, like checking their mail and stepping over me. No one's helping me up. And I'm yelling. Somebody must a called EMS, 'cause about forty-five minutes later these two black dudes show up and throw me into the back of this stinking van somebody must a died in there. Lots a people probably died in there come to think of it.

So they like take me to the ER. Kinda drop me off on account of I could walk on one leg. I guess if you've got uncontrollable bleeding from a head wound or some shit like that, then they put you on a stretcher. Me they just dumped.

So I'm in the ER, and they're cutting my pants off and I'm still stoned so I'm trying to tell 'em to gimme my wallet but no one's listening to me, they're just like dressing me up in these blue pants I got on now and they're saying shit like, "Why did you break your leg? Why did you break your leg? Don't you know you're HIV-positive and you could've gotten a life-threatening infection?" Like I do it all the time. Like it's my fuckin' hobby.

And this doctor comes in, right outta a med school. Clean, you know the type, young, serious. Probably got an A average in dissection class. Plays a mean game a racquetball. Probably does seven hundred pushups every morning and smokes cigars while he's doin' 'em. And he looks at my chart and says, "Why did you break your leg, you're HIV-positive? You could get an infection and die." And I get a little animated you know. And then he says, "Calm down, I know how you feel."

I said, "Hey. You don't know how I feel." And he says, "Yes I do." Like he does. And I lose it. I start yelling and I try to get off the gurney, and somebody pushes me back down and I push them away and I threw this roll of bandages and this bed pan and uh . . . well they got these bouncers at St. Vincent's now.

And they threw me out on the street, they wouldn't let me back in. And I'm standing there out in the snow, blue-green hospital pants, this walking cast thing. I don't have my wallet, I don't have anything, I'm just standin' there and this little old lady, saw me standing there and she lays a fiver on me. Says, "God bless you."

So I comes home. And all the food was cold and coagulated. So I gave it to Snowball, who's thinking, This is my lucky day. And I'm thinking, When's mine?

From **31 EJACULATIONS**
No. 19

So I'm walking around the apartment nude, my erection waving in front of me like a divining rod. It was sure to stay rock hard for a while since I had about fourteen rubber bands wrapped tightly around its base. I could see the shaft was turning purple. Only problem was, now I needed something to shove up my a-hole. And finding the right item was mildly embarrassing since I had to search all over the bungalow and I don't keep any curtains on my windows. I know the woman across the way sits in the darkness and watches me. She works for an executive at a movie studio down in Culver City, so keeping an eye on me is probably the most fun she has all day. I should send her a bill.

I was on a mission. Find something longer than it was wide. Door handle, no good. Bicycle pump, too painful. Small vase, too wide. And then I remembered: old faithful . . . vegetation. I mean you really have to wonder why God made all these vegetables in the form they take. And indeed, I was in luck, a bag of organic carrots was nestled behind a six-pack of soy milk on the bottom of the fridge. I selected a nice thick one and I was all set. A little Vaseline daubed on for comfort and—uhhhhhh!—rock 'n' roll!

Now I was in fine shape, looking good! Rubber bands strangling my dick, clothes pins on my nipples, a freshly shaved head and a carrot up my ass. Time to get busy. A little Oil of Olay on the old helmet, buff, buff, buff, bring it up to speed. Oh yeah. Feeling fresh. Get out that hash pipe packed with Maui bud. Um-hmmm, here we go. Like a mallet beating a xylophone, that THC strokes up the cocaine percolating through my bloodstream. I'd try another hit right now, but shooting up with a carrot in your ass can be dangerous. Sit down too fast you could rupture something. So I take a sip of a Starbucks triple espresso. Gone cold, but I'm beyond temperature. Time to fly! Polish, polish, polish . . . oh yeah . . . memories coming up, dimly, faster, stronger: playing doctor behind the shed; getting pissed on for the first time . . . and now . . . oh yeah, where am I? Living room, get into the bathroom, quick! Oh yeah, oh yeah, there it is, the noose, my lover, over the door. The noose, the noose. Just get my smooth head in there. Quick, the train's coming into the station!!! Oh yeah, and nudge that carrot. Uh-huh. Here we go, coming, gonna come, get it tight around the neck, now DROP . . .

GATED

Happy guy bent down, talking to a child.

What's your name? Jimmy? Hi, Jimmy. I'm Bill. And how old are you? Seven!! That's pretty big! Are you all excited about looking for a new house with Mommy and Daddy? You're not? Why? Who's Jeremy? Is Jeremy your best friend? He is? Well, when you move here you're going to make lots of new friends. Better friends. See that lady over there? Her name is Sandy and she's going to give you one of our special lollipops.

(Standing up straight.)

Nice kid. Chip? Cathi? Before we look at the model home, let's just go over some of the things we said on the phone. First of all when you buy here at Cedar Woods Community Estates, the maintenance is paid for for the first year. That would cover upkeep of the grounds, the tennis courts, the swimming pool, the guards at the front gate and the K-9 patrols. And of course, the school, which Jimmy will be able to enter next year. Uh, no. The school is just for residents. Local townspeople are not allowed within the perimeter of the complex at any time. And . . . yes, oh, I almost forgot, the medical center is also here, if Jimmy falls off the bike—which is about the worst thing that can happen here. I tell you, I've been living here for five years, and the place is so quiet: no traffic, no sirens at night, no screams, no gunshots.

Now, our only requirement is no pets. No dogs, no cats, no gerbils, no Vietnamese pot belly pigs. Fish? Of course you can have fish, as long as they're under four inches. We choose the color of your house. Don't want any paisley houses. No more than two children per family here. Big families are not conducive to the kind of environment Cedar Woods Estates wants to foster. You've got Jimmy, so you can have one more.

And you have to be employed. You guys are all set, we did a little checking. Chip, we heard about your promotion and everyone is so excited. As long as you maintain employment you'll have no problems. If you're not employed for whatever reason you get put on a list and it's possible you'd . . . it's no big deal . . . you'd have to be unemployed for over a year for it to mean anything. And that's not going to happen.

You cannot receive any kind of welfare payments. You can get medicaid, social security, stuff like that. But we don't want anyone to live here who is on welfare for obvious reasons. It's one of the rules that work very well for us.

Now this development is in the new section, like I said, the old section is five years old. Everything here will be just like the original. Except that we will be installing security cameras every one hundred feet along all the streets. It's kind of an experiment. Some of the houses will have sensors right inside the walls. Only if you want them. See how it works.

I think security is really the biggest factor for most people. People want to live somewhere safe, where they can be happy. And that's what we provide. All our security guards are ex-LAPD, great bunch of guys. All licensed to carry automatic weapons, tasers and mace. No . . . no pepper spray. Mace. Real mace. It's the little things.

Not only are we looking for crime since there's no crime here, we don't want anyone unusual in the area either. Our guys see somebody walking around who doesn't belong here, they stop 'em, they question 'em and they escort them off the premises.

This is not a racial thing, we have many black families (not that many). And some Asian families. Very nice, you'd be surprised. (Well actually just one.)

We have our own recycling center, we don't want anybody picking up cans, going door to door or asking for anything. We don't allow solicitation of any kind. Stop 'em right at the gate. We do our own fundraising every Christmas. Linda, where'd we send the money last year? Oh right, the displaced Costa Rican coffee farmers. Great cause. Because we don't just see this as a bunch of buildings, we see this as a living opportunity.

Which brings me to my favorite thing, the civic association. Now if you own a home here you are automatically a member of the civic association. But if you pay a small dues every year, I dunno, it's something like twenty bucks, they just add it to your maintenance, then you can be a certified member. And I would recommend that. You get a newsletter, we have our annual meetings, rallies, those kinds of things. The ones at night with the bonfires are a lot of fun. And you get to put a little plaque by your front door so that all your neighbors know you're a certified member in good standing: you know, you've paid your maintenance, you're employed, no fish over four inches. You even get a pin, see? Nice huh? In fact, we require that you wear it. Jimmy, how would you like to have a pin? It'll match the uniform all the little guys get to wear. Armbands and everything!

You know, you're gonna love it here, Jimmy. On Halloween, we all go door to door and everybody gives nice treats—no fishhooks in the apples, no rat poison. On Christmas, Santa comes to visit and we all go Christmas caroling. We're thankful because everything here is the way it's supposed to be. So whaddya say, Chip? Cathi? Jimmy? Let's go see that model home.

PAIN RELIEVER

Hi! Like most people I have the kind of job that stresses me out twenty-four-seven/three-sixty-five. And after five cups of coffee I get a headache that feels like someone's driving nails into my skull with a sledgehammer. I used to think there was nothing I could do. I tried aspirin, Tylenol, Excedrin, even Extra Strength Advil—nothing worked. I'd writhe in agony at my desk all day and lie awake all night. That was before I discovered something that works better, lasts longer and lets me get the rest I need so I wake up refreshed in the morning ready to hit that traffic jam—heroin. Taken daily, heroin gets rid of my headaches like *no other* pain reliever. Ten milligrams in the morning, ten milligrams at night and my pain is *gone*. Heroin—the modern pain reliever. *(New, snappier voice) And next time, instead of those five cups of coffee, try crack—the quicker picker-upper.*

WOOD (X-MAS TREE)

I want *wood*. I want to live near woods. Trees. And I want to burn wood in a fireplace and sit in front of it. And have a rocking chair made of real wood. Maybe a pipe made out of wood. And all this wood will make me feel nostalgic for the olden days when things were only made of wood. No plastic. No styrofoam. Just wood. Wooden wheels rolling over the prairie. Log cabins. Made of wood. And wool. A wool comforter and a good book. Falling asleep over a good book in front of a roaring fire. Of wood.

When you get older you become nostalgic, just like when you're young you keep thinking about the future and how great it's going to be. Then you get there and it's not so great, so you switch over to thinking about how great everything used to be.

It works like this: first you're little and you're very excited about everything, and everything is very important and you feel somewhat safe; then you get older and you think you know everything and you take chances; then you get disappointed and realize you're getting older and things don't feel safe at all; then you are even older and cherish any day in which you don't have aches and pains; then you die.

I think I understood how it all works when I was about three years old. It was the fifties. I was three in the fifties. It was Christmas, an old-fashioned Christmas. Eisenhower was president, everything was completely depressing, the war had been over only a few years, even the stock market crash hadn't been that long ago. People just getting over their last bout of polio . . .

And I'm three, and all of a sudden one day I toddle out to the living room, and for some reason my parents, who up to now have seemed pretty unremarkable, have chopped down a tree and dragged it into the house. Not just any tree but a cone-shaped, very green, nicely smelly tree. And I like this. I like having a tree in the house. This could start a trend, bring a tree into the house, then a bush, maybe a cow, a horse, who knows? I can dig it. And then, even cooler, they get all these colored lights and glass balls and shiny tinsel and throw it all over the tree. Cool. Very cool. A side of my parents I have not seen before. Colors. Shiny shit. So I'm happy. I think, maybe this isn't going to be so bad living with these people.

And they seemed to be into it, too, taking pictures of me in front of the tree, laughing, singing songs about stars and bells and angels, very cool imagery. And I'm blissed out—we get presents, nuts, oranges, chocolate, happy people all around.

So every morning, first thing, I run out to the living room and yup, it's still there, the tree. And I just sit there and groove to this tree. Develop a relationship with the tree. Even gave it a name—Larry—Larry the tree.

And then one day I come out to find my dad taking all the decorations off Larry. And I go, "Whoa! Like what are you doing to my friend?" And my mom is standing there and she says, "Larry has to go back to the forest. Christmas is over."

And then my dad, who has always been neurotically committed to being honest, especially when it causes other people pain, says, "Larry's not going back to the forest." And he pulls out this ax and starts chopping up the tree!

I'm in shock.

I say, "But what's going to happen to Larry?" And my mom says, "Well . . ." And I say, "So where's he going?" Dad says, "Either it'll get burned up in a giant bonfire someplace," which of course stuns me to hear this about someone I've gotten very close to, "or . . ." (now check this out) "it'll get ground into mulch and be made into paper." I ask, "What kind of paper?" and my dad says, "I don't know, toilet paper maybe." Toilet paper. My best friend in the whole world is getting ground into toilet paper!

I was traumatized and to this day, every time I wipe my ass I think of Christmas.

BUILDING CHARACTER

MY METHOD FOR CREATING THE SOLOS

In 1980 I wrote and performed a piece called *Men Inside*. It wasn't "stand-up comedy" or a "showcase" or "performance art." It was a play for one person. I had no intention of ever making another like it. I couldn't imagine that this initial exercise would morph into a series of solos that I (and others) would perform in venues across the United States and the world. *Wake Up and Smell the Coffee* is the sixth in this series of full-length solos. When I created *Wake Up*, I put it together pretty much the same way I did when I made *Men Inside* twenty years before. What follows is a description of how I first came to make these solos and my method for making them.

—

Around 1978, having arrived in New York three years earlier, I met the actor David Warrilow, a charter member of the Mabou Mines theatre company. He had the most perfect speaking voice, so I asked him for some actorly advice on how to improve mine. He told me to get a tape recorder, tape my voice and listen to the results. He said I could be my own teacher.

I bought a cheap plastic cassette recorder and taped some off-the-cuff ramblings. I wasn't working off any particular text or play, so I improvised as I spoke. For instance, I'd "do" a southern-style voice. I didn't try for any specific dialect, I was just screwing around. I'd launch into a Sam Shepardesque monologue about fast cars and guns and liquor without thinking too much about what I was saying. The words flowed.

Later, when I listened to the tape I realized I had been improvising a little monologue. I hadn't consciously planned to create a character but someone waiting inside me had spoken up.

I made more tapes. As these improvs mounted up, I decided to catalog the "people who live inside me." I sorted them out and came up with twelve distinct male archetypes, ranging from a threatening street punk ("Nice Shoes") to a redneck deer hunter ("Rodeo") to a little boy playing ("Superman!"). All of these characters were the product of free-form vocal improv. I wasn't looking "out there" for characters, I was looking "inside."

This gallery of characters, this set of monologues, became *Men Inside*. I performed it first in 1980 at Franklin Furnace, a small loft space. Lots of people (fifty?) showed up and dug it. Later (after touring and playing clubs for two years), I performed it in a more polished version, at Joe Papp's New York Shakespeare Festival.

By then, I had become an exile from the traditional theatre (I had come to New York with a theatre degree, planning to work Off-Broadway), making performance pieces and performing them in lofts and back rooms. Other pieces like *Careful Movement* (performed at St. Mark's Poetry Project) and *Garden* (Artists Space) featured a few actors spouting chunks of text, some taped voices and slides. I also wrote "plays" like *Sheer Heaven* (at The Kitchen, performed entirely in Spanish for English-speaking audiences) and *The New World* (featuring fourteen actors and music by Glenn

Branca). I had a nightclub act (*The Ricky Paul Show*) in which I played an obnoxious comedian who sang off-key and hurled insults at the audience.

During the *Ricky* show, fights would break out with the audience, sometimes bottles got thrown. I went to Berlin and goose-stepped onstage. In New York, an enraged feminist tried to throw me down a flight of stairs because I made bad jokes about women's lib. I was always booed and hissed. Gigs were canceled because my stuff was thought to be in poor taste or too violent or *negative*! I didn't care. The energy was exciting. In my own awkward way, I was trying to make a new kind of anti-theatre.

I hung-out at places like CBGB's, Max's, The Mudd Club and Hurrah's. I embraced a "punk" aesthetic. I liked the energy. Aggressive and loud. Antagonistic to the status quo, it didn't take itself too seriously, it liked to laugh. There was a new attitude in the music that said awkward was good, grotesque was fascinating. Punk was rough, it didn't smooth everything into lovely shapes.

In punk music, the chords were basic. I wanted to do the same thing with performance—make stuff that was straightforward, not precious, not effete. (I became a fan of Richard Foreman's Ontological-Hysteric Theater. His work was super-energized, sexual, multilayered to the point of madness, awkward, funny, beautifully designed and way too loud for most people.)

As fun as it was, by 1981 I had reached a point when I had to fish or cut bait. The plays, subsidized with my paycheck from The Kitchen, were not getting reviewed and they were expensive. I couldn't afford to do them anymore (I paid the actors, paid for rehearsal space, made the posters and sets myself, etc.). And as much as I loved the punk club lifestyle (late nights in the demimonde, the frenzy of the shows, harsh personalities, beer-stink dressing rooms replete with cracked mirrors), *Ricky* was a one-trick pony.

So when the opportunity came up for me to tour as a solo act with a group of other performers, including the original

Rock Steady Crew and Fab Five Freddy (the first rap/break-dance/deejay gang to hit the Midwest), I grabbed it. I decided *Men Inside* was the best piece to do. While on tour, one venue billed me as a "comedian." Because the audience expected to laugh, they did.

I liked this. I liked the idea of acting-out a dozen obnoxious characters, pissing off the audience but drawing them in as well. I liked the energy level of solo, it felt limitless. I kept working on the characters, refining them, giving them more dimension, finding the comedic beats, the aggressive beats.

I decided to focus my attention on my solo work, treating the pieces as one-person plays. I wasn't always sure where I was going with the new material, but to paraphrase Wallace Shawn: "I find out what I want to write about by writing it."

———

I want to get theoretical here for a page or two and discuss acting and character and, ultimately, writing for the stage, at least as it applies to what I do.

Theatre is character, everything else is window-dressing. It's not the terrific story that makes Shakespeare great, it's the characters. It's not the atmosphere that makes the Greek tragedies awesome, it's the characters. And the same is true with Ibsen, Chekhov, Williams. (The exceptions might be Beckett and Pinter. Maybe.)

What makes a character tick is fascinating because we are all characters in the way we see ourselves and the way we see others. "Character" is our way of conceptualizing who we are. Character is what we create every time we interact with another. In his book, *The Presentation of Self in Everyday Life*, Erving Goffman says we learn how to *act* to be the people we are. "Acting" in day-to-day life is more than behaving, it is imitating, it is constructing. When I am interacting with other people, I am consciously or unconsciously imitating the behavior of other people I've known. And to take it one step further, because I live in a world of mass media, I experience all sorts of people who are not only in my life but who I "know" from movies or TV.

A doctor models his behavior after other doctors. A truck driver behaves like a truck driver because he's shown that he can act a certain way. In fact, if you visited the doctor and he behaved like a truck driver (gruff, for example), you'd wonder what sort of doctor he was. We tell each other who we are through our behavior. Not only do we hone our behavior according to the role we are playing in society, we spend a lot of time fine-tuning our act, especially in dynamic social situations, like trying to get laid or doing business. This information about how I *should* behave is not innate, it comes from outside myself.

I consider this when playing a part. For example, I am given the role of a soldier (Buchner's *Woyzeck*). I have no "sense memory" of being a soldier. I *do* have the memory of being in fist fights or being hurt or being scared. And, of course, when I act, I access those feelings. But I also have a memory of soldiers and how soldiers behave in the dozens of war movies I've seen, not to mention TV. So, in fact, I'm recalling a memory of an actor playing a soldier. And that's as real as anything else in life as far as my subconscious is concerned. The point isn't to replicate life on stage but, as Picasso said, "create a lie that tells the truth." And truth is what everybody agrees truth is.

We all have little theatres in our respective heads. The whole world is replicated in our minds. The way we imagine ourselves and other people is a cornerstone to the way we act in our daily lives. We make representations of people mentally and play out imaginary scenes with these imaginary people. From these mental exercises we feel we can predict how someone (say, our mother or father) will behave, and we act accordingly. The interesting thing is that the mother in my head has just as much to do with the real person as she does with the way I think about her. People are conceptual.

The goal of the theatre artist is to take the imaginary "mother" and put her on stage in such a way that when other people come to see the play, they see a mother they recognize. If an audience doesn't *recognize* what they see, then the play doesn't work. The audience sees things laid-out in front of them and they compare the mechanisms of behavior (the acting, the behaving, the plot) to the way they think about them, as opposed to the way they "really" are, which is unknowable.

Theatre is powerful because it works in exact concordance with the way our heads work (not the way reality works). To quote Samuel Johnson (via Harold Bloom in *Shakespeare: The Invention of the Human*): "Imitations produce pain or pleasure not because they are mistaken for realities but because they bring realities to mind." The truthfulness of the theatre is determined by the audience. Theatre is consensus. And that consensus is a function of characters who speak and act the way characters in our collective head speak and act. In other words: archetypes. Success can only be measured by the ratio of what I (the artist) see, versus what the audience thinks they see. Marcel Duchamp, a great lover of science, suggested this ratio. He said the closer to one-to-one this ratio becomes, the greater the artist. But of course, no one can measure such a ratio.

People don't remember what happened in life, they remember what they *think* happened. People don't see things, they see what they *think* they see. And they don't know people, they know what they *think* they know. To tangle with all that thinking, well, that's what art is all about. Effective art agitates the certainty that what you know is the truth. Art turns things upside-down and inside-out.

———

So enough theory. Here's how I make a solo. I start with a tape recorder and an empty room. I work in a space where I'm completely isolated and no one can overhear me. And I make sure there's enough room to bounce around. When I'm alone, I can let go and fantasize without self-consciousness. I can improvise freely, become the character and let him loose. Self-consciousness ruins creativity. I turn on the tape recorder, I note the date and the piece I'm working on. Then I start.

Once I get a chunk of improv down, I review the tape and try to find parts I like the sound of. I transcribe these. I keep collections of these transcriptions and revisit them later. Then I select pieces from the transcription that I like, sample them and commit them to memory. I then use these segments as a launch pad for another improv. Then I start the process all over again. The final edited piece of monologue is maybe three minutes long, after hours of improvs.

Good things happen when I do it this way. First of all, when I'm speaking I'm looser with language than when I write. There isn't as much editorializing going on. Secondly, the arc of the story of the finished monologue (and every monologue has a beginning, middle and an end) is not as predictable. This is the way people talk. They wander, they get interrupted, they think of ancillary ideas as they speak, they listen to the other person and react.

In my daily life, I overhear all kinds of conversations: people discussing or gossiping about their friends, lunatics shouting out at passersby, people swearing at each other from their cars, people sitting at a meal, lovers arguing on a subway platform, me yelling at my own children. When I hear something interesting, I note it, and I might use it later as a starting point for an improv.

When I begin the improv with a fragment of overheard speech, I repeat it like a mantra, using the phrase to invoke an attitude. For example, take the phrase: "Fuck you!" The improv might go something like:

"Fuck you." "Fuck *you!*" "No, man, fuck *you!*" "You saying, 'Fuck you!' to me? Well fuck you!" "Come here and say that." "No, you come here." "I'll come there if you come here." "What, you're telling me what to do now? You think you're better than me?" "As a matter of fact I do, shithead." "Who you calling a 'shithead'? Fuck you!" Etc.

In "Upgrade" from *Wake Up*, I riff on the kind of officious check-in counterperson. The key word here is "sir."

Here you go, sir, you're all set. You have a seat on this flight, it's leaving in ten minutes so you better hurry up! Yes, sir, that's right, it's a coach seat. Yes, I know you had a fully-paid-for-first-class ticket, sir, but this seat is coach. Well, let me see what I can do, OK? *(Types into keyboard)* Alright, I'm looking at a first-class seat on a 3:30 A.M. departure with a six-hour layover in Saint Louis. How's that sound?

Yes, 3:30 in the morning, sir, that's correct. I understand that, sir. Yes, I can see that you have a gold card. All the people behind you have gold cards, sir. Well, sir, sir, sir, why don't we do this: step aside for a sec here, let me get everyone on board, get them seated, let the flight leave and then we can see what we can do, OK? *(Signals to next person)* Next in line?

The trick with these improvs is not to aim for anything in particular. Not to try to make it funny or poignant. I just want to become the person behind the counter and get into the situation and see what happens from there. The most important goal is to play and cut loose, to let the character speak for himself. This is not the time to worry about final performance, how inarticulate or articulate the character sounds.

Here is a fragment of the verbatim transcript of the first improv I did for *Wake Up*'s "Harmonious":

What do we learn from this story? [I've just finished telling a story about a farmer who has a pig with one leg. The story was not included in the final piece.] That we are either in harmony or we are in dis-equlibrium and alienation. So let us make a list in our minds: what are the things that make us happy, what are the things that make us sad. Happy? Buying a new car. Sad: doing our taxes. Happy: swimming in our swimming pool. Sad: paying the doctor's bills. Happy: being on vacation. Sad: having to go to work. If we look at these things and we understand what they are telling us, we find a deep spiritual principle coming into play. And that is this: alienation is simply a lack of money. If we have money we don't have these problems. So our first goal is to make sure that we understand that money is the thing we must have above all.

The final script goes like this:

The second thing you must understand is that we exist in two states. We are either in sync with the universe or we are out of sync with the universe. When we are in sync with the universe, we call this being *harmonious*. When we are out of sync with the universe, we call this being *alienated*.

We are either in sync or out of sync, harmonious or alienated. How do we know which state we are in? *(Pause, smiles, shrugs shoulders)* We just know!

So let us now clear our minds and still our centers. And let us contemplate these two states of being—harmony and alienation:

I am warm, I am happy, I am harmonious.
I am cold, I am angry, I am alienated.

> I am swimming in my heated swimming pool.
> I am harmonious.
> I am doing my taxes. I am alienated.
> I am buying a brand-new Lexus with all-leather
> interior. I am harmonious.
> I am working three jobs to pay for health insur-
> ance. I am alienated.
> I am flying first class to Saint Bart's. I am har-
> monious.
> I am going to jail for food stamp fraud. I am
> alienated.

If we carefully meditate upon these two states of being, we find a deep and abiding spiritual principle becomes obvious:

Alienation is simply a lack of money.

And, of course, the corollary:

Money brings deep and abiding harmony.

When we have money, our days are full of sunshine, the air is fresh and clean. We love everyone we meet. And everyone loves us.

When we lack money, we become empty and angry. We listen to overly loud music. And we are frequently constipated.

And so each and every one of us is on a path and must answer the eternal question: "How do I get more money?"

This is the path that I am on. That is why you are here tonight.

I move from the original to the final version through tran-scription, memorization, repeated rehearsals, discussions with my director, live "workshop" performances and performances as part of the run, as well as touring. Every time I perform the piece, I look to see if its logic, tone, humor and rhythm are what I want them to be. Coincidentally, the more consistent and clear the piece becomes, the easier it is to memorize and perform.

Another way into the character during the improv phase is to find a physical aspect of the character and work with that. The way a junkie lights a cigarette for instance, nodding into the flame as he tries to puff. That can get me started. The way someone holds a beer bottle or a coffee cup. The way an old man might shuffle across a room (*Wake Up*'s "The Meeting"). At one point in Danny Hoch's great solo piece *Jails, Hospitals and Hip-Hop*, he sweeps a floor with a push broom. We see the anger with every swipe.

Finally, and most powerfully, would be to assume a vocal stance. Not outward mimicry, because mimicry is hollow, but letting the vocal posture shape the improv from within. Try reciting "The Gettysburg Address" in a Minnie Mouse voice and you'll get the idea. The medium is the message.

Taking a piece of the character, a way of speaking or a posture, or a vocal intonation sets me on the path. From this beginning, the world of the character can be discovered and a story line develop. (To see where all this might lead, check out "Our Gang" or "Stag Party," two earlier monologues from *Drinking in America* and *Sex, Drugs, Rock & Roll*.)

Harking back to the way we perform in everyday life, behavior in front of an audience is always performance, no matter who the audience is: a teacher addressing a class, a preacher preaching, a trainer running a gym class or a lunatic on the street. So I collect these natural situations for performance and use them to launch an improv. (I was influenced here by the late great Brother Theodore, whose whack comedic rants were in the guise of a sermon.) This is one place when in film actors cross over into the truly theatrical. Check out Burt Lancaster in *Elmer Gantry* or Alec Baldwin in *Glengarry Glen Ross*. Public figures make great performances; public speeches are an easy way to work with themes. In my first show, I played a preacher giving a sermon in "Looking Out for Number One." He was enormously fun to play. The new age guru in "Harmonious" does the same thing.

This guru, like many characters I play, says the opposite of what you expect. This is a writing device, akin to playing devil's advocate, which I use in a lot of what I do. I can't think of anything more boring than telling the audience what "I really think" because, in fact, I'm not sure myself. Likewise, I want my characters to be unexpected and fresh. Playing against the grain of expectation is one way of doing this.

And I want the character to make a point. There's usually some angle I want to get at with each monologue within a show. For example, I may want to show how even the biggest jerk has *his* side of the story. Like in "Breakthrough" *(Wake Up)*:

Well, I took the boys to the ball game. Oh yeah, it was fun. They're so great. Acting up, throwin' Cracker Jacks at each other. Yelling, screaming. And I'm like, "Hey! Hey! Hey! Quiet the fuck DOWN! RIGHT! NOW!" I'm so good with those guys, you know? Oh! Oh! And this busybody behind me is like, "Stop yelling at your kids, I'm trying to hear the game." And I'm dealing with boundary issues today, like we've been working on, so I'm like, "Are these *your* kids? Or are these *my* kids?" Right? "You don't hear me telling you to put a bag on your wife's head 'cause she's so fuckin' ugly."

And from this, the guy gets an attitude. You know? All indignant. Gets in my face. Now I'm in a fight. How did this happen? And I can walk away, I can walk away. But I have my needs today. And I've learned to respect my needs. And my need was to punch him in the face, so I did.

I want the character to feel like a living being to the audience. Ninety-nine percent of this is intuition and can't be taught. Scientific accuracy won't make a more compelling character on stage. (Although research might make a more grounded actor.) For me, being somewhere safe where I can improvise helps me find this intuition. I want the character to be energetic, to be worth watching. One way of looking at this is to imagine performing in front of an audience that doesn't speak the character's language. Would these people, who don't understand a word, still find what's happening on stage worth watching? With that in mind, I try to create characters who are active—standing, moving, engaged. I stay away from mime because I find mime (and costumes) distracting for an audience. I want the essence of the character, not the hat. I don't want the audience judging me on how well I mime driving a car.

Characters in my shows vary in how broad I play them. A broadly played character, played for laughs, very declaratory, is a "sketch" character, like what you might see on *Saturday Night Live*. But characters can also be so intense they frighten the audience (because they are so believable). Or they can be so grounded, the audience forgets that they are watching an actor. I make use of all of these approaches when acting, because they are all part of the world of pretending to be someone else. The only question I can't answer is: "What is good acting?"

Another monologue I do is called a rant. It's a direct, emphatic, not quite logical address to the audience with some sort of theme. Here, the character I'm playing is me. But, of course, once on stage, there's no such thing as "me," there's only character. I started doing stuff like this back when I did the *Ricky Paul Show*. I would go ballistic and rant about women, life in the city, injustice, etc. Later I played with the rant as Barry in the play *Talk Radio*. In the "rant" mode, I discover voices of characters who live within me, not so much as archetypes, but as purified attitude. Usually this attitude is anger.

I made a commitment to this mode of monologue when Jo Bonney, my director, latched onto a stream-of-consciousness essay I had written on a night when I was feeling very frustrated and poverty-stricken. It was called "Dog Chameleon." I told her it didn't fit in the show we were working on at the time (*Sex, Drugs, Rock & Roll*), it wasn't a bona fide character. She said try it anyway. Today, I think it's my favorite piece from that show because it flows with great rhythm, it speaks from a hidden part of me (so it's embarrassing) and it's funny. It's also not so easy to play, it requires concentration. "The Glass" in *Pounding Nails in the Floor with My Forehead*, all the "Intros" and "The Ladder" in *Wake Up* fall into the rant category:

And sure, maybe I'll have to step on a few people as I make my way to the top. But every head I step on will be just another rung in the ladder of fame and fortune. Because I'm honest with myself. Let's face it, we're all on a ladder, from the lowliest beggar in Calcutta all the way up to Steven Spielberg, we all have our place. And it takes guts, it takes willpower and vision to reach up to that next rung and drag myself up. And sure when I get to the top, maybe all my friends will hate me but by then I'll have new friends. Better friends. *Everyone* will be my friend!

People will line up just to hang out with me, even my parents! They'll be like Mary and Joseph standing by the manger when all the kings came by. Puffed-up with pride like blowfish. And I'll be like baby Jesus, a godlet, on the straw for all to admire!

And when my new friends come by to visit, we'll be happy. We'll be happy together because now we can do what we've always wanted to do: just hang out all day

and think and talk about *ME*! Interviews with me!
Photo calls with me! Me! Me! Me!

And when I get tired of my new friends, I'll say good
night, climb into my king-sized four-poster bed, snuggle under the covers and pull out the remote control,
and as my eyes slowly close, there I am again. On E!
I'm on E! I'm on *Charlie Rose*. I'm on *Conan*! I'm on
Leno! I'm a VH-1 veejay! I'm EVERYWHERE!

I'm *ubiquitous*! *(Becomes transformed, rising to his
full height, arms out, emanating power)* God-like, like
the sun, my rays shining down on every surface of the
earth! My tentacles entwined around every mind, every
imagination! *(Audience member on his knees in awe)*
"What is it like to be *him*?" *(Triumphant)* That's what
they'll all want to know!

Of course I'm playing a character. I'm playing an "Eric"
who lives in my head. To improvise a character like this is
almost like doing therapy because a hidden part of my per-
sonality is being put before the audience. I'm exposing
myself. Often I get there just by pacing back and forth in my
studio, saying the first thing that comes to mind (and taping
it). If I'm really honest, some interesting stuff can emerge.

Once I get a pile of monologues together, I begin to think
about the order of the show. Like a play, the show must have
a beginning, a middle and an end. Each show must have a
certain urgency that makes the audience interested in what
comes next. To this end, each monologue within a show is
serving various purposes:

1. It's got to be worth watching in and of itself. In other
   words, if I were to do this piece without the rest of the
   show, is it an interesting piece of theatre? Does it have
   themes, humor, characterization and physicality that
   work, whether or not it fits into the larger context?

2. Does the piece connect to the overall theme? I don't care if the theme is obvious or not, or if it's only meaningful to me, but there has to be a connection. The show might be about power. What does this particular segment say about power? Am I repeating myself, is there another segment that says the same thing?

3. How does the piece relate to the rhythm of the whole show? It's important to vary the pace of the show. I'm not going to do a really loud, maddened bit and follow it with another just like it. And varying intensity and tempo is not just a matter of ups and downs. The intensity and tempo of a piece tell the audience where we are in the show. "The Highway" in *Wake Up*, with its dark mood and spooky references to the future, is one way to end the show.

4. Since the monologue's position in the show is relative to the structure of the show, does it build on what's come before it? It may act as an overture, a pause in the middle, comic relief, a summation or something else. The introduction in the beginning of *Wake Up* is typical for me. I make claims the show will trigger insight in the audience. I imply the show will change the audience's life. I'm letting the audience know that this is not a show in which they can just sit back and yuck it up.

I might put irritating, offensive stuff pretty early in the show as a way of saying: You're either with me or not; You wanna come along? "Faith" in *Wake Up* works this way by presenting the audience with a garish account of Jesus' crucifixion:

. . . So, what happens? The old man in the sky, *Daddy*, took little Jesus, His son, nailed his skinny butt to a piece of wood in the middle of the desert so a bunch of jerk-offs could check him out like some kind of rotisserie chicken at the Safeway.

Later, I lighten up the mood with simpler material like "Harmonious," the send-up of the self-help guru. In both cases, I am opening up themes that are important to the show (the arbitrary nature of God, the belief that money is everything), but it's *how* I open them up that lays out the parameters of the show. I keep the audience guessing: "Is this guy serious?" Behind all the characters, there is the character the audience is most curious about, Eric Bogosian.

Toward the end of the show, I will present the more complex pieces, when the accretion of what I'm saying has built into a larger theme (and so eventually the whole show). In *Wake Up* this section of the show begins with "The Ladder" and extends through "The Meeting," "Sheep," and finally ends with "The Highway." Once I've got the audience following me down the "devil's advocate" path, I start throwing the bigger themes into the air and juggling them, ideas about ambition, hypocrisy and, ultimately, how alone and impotent I feel in the face of these conflicting urges. All of this doesn't have to add up to something as coherent as a thesis. I don't have to be making a particular point, I can, and do, simply meditate on a theme, or ask a question. In "The Highway," I say that since there's nothing that can be done about any of this, we might as well walk into the woods and die. (Do I believe any of this? A part of me does.)

I can't use all the material I create in the improvs. I may like something that might not work in the context of the larger show. When I was working on *Wake Up*, I created a character who was kind of a junkie ("Victim," included here in the "Orphans" section). I couldn't find a way to use him in the show. At the same time, I continued to work on another character, someone in therapy ("Toxic"). Eventually I merged the sense of the two in "Breakthrough," creating a character who is in therapy but obviously not getting anywhere fast, but thinks he is.

For me, characters are not static, set creations, they are more like quantum particle clouds of behavior, attitudes, statements. One character merges into the next. Characters are contrivances, synthesized from my mind, my imagination. There is no outside objective reality with which to compare them. Ultimately, a "good" character is the one who possesses the most force. So I will borrow and steal and experiment until I cobble together a character who has the most "truth." It's like each character is a small universe and must work according to his own laws of physics. I experiment, like Frankenstein, until I get the character who sits up and lives.

As I rewrite and polish, rehearse and perform, I am honing facets of the piece: rhythm, humor, character, pace, verbal imagery, even theme. Once I know I'll be keeping a monologue in a piece, I try to take it to another level. The words must be organized in almost a rhythm, the music of the words. The way words run along on top of one another is, for me, part of the pleasure of performing. Finding the right combination takes time and rehearsal.

An example would be the middle of "Intro" in *Wake Up*:

Until one day, the sun warms us and we melt. We become a trickle, the trickle becomes a stream, the stream a river, as we reunite with all the other little drops and become a mighty torrent. Powerful, roaring, cascading—we are the *Ganges*—yes! Immense, pouring down into the valley. Full of life and energy and *fish*! People are swimming in us! Laughing, joking!!!

Elephants squirt arcing sprays from their trunks! Shamans baptize their followers in our sacred waters! Dark-eyed women scrub their washing on the rocks, pounding their dhotis and saris with sticks, the water droplets splashing joyously up into the air! Even the

dead are brought to us upon their fiery funeral pyres,
as they say their final good-bye to this transient life.
People chant! They sing! They celebrate! We are the
river, we are life itself! We are HOLY!

In order to perform this with the most impact, I have to
know where all my breaths will lie and where the emphasis
will be hit squarely. I find these rhythms through trial and
error. Finding the metaphors that work with the river image,
the right pictures of joyous Indians bathing in holy waters, all
this comes from the polishing period of the piece. The writing has been carried a long way from the initial improv. This
happens during rehearsals with Jo.

Live performance, trial and error, get the humor and pace
right. Humor is a matter of taste. What makes me laugh isn't
necessarily going to make *you* laugh. Laughter is perhaps the
hardest element to control. And laughter works differently in
a theatre than in other art forms, because there are always
some people who "get it" and trigger other people. And there
are those who "don't" and act as a brake. Again, consensus
rules.

Verbal imagery is a matter of moving away from the predictable. I'm making pictures in the audience's mind with
words. The right word or phrase conjures a mental image by
being fresh and on the money. Often I find the right image in
performance when I'm not thinking too hard about it. This is
another factor that gets tuned up when I'm doing shows at
places like Performance Space 122 or the Knitting Factory,
where I'm very comfortable.

I keep polishing with Jo in rehearsal. This is a matter of
continuing to look at the basic character I'm playing and asking fundamental questions that the initial improvs may have
missed. For instance, "What was this character doing ten
minutes ago?" "What is the character wearing, carrying?"
"How old is this character, how does that affect his voice,

posture?" "Are we outdoors? Is it warm? Cold?" And so on. These are almost standard acting class questions, but they work to jog my imagination, helping me find a new way to approach the material. Finally, there is just a question of right-ness: what feels right and what feels wrong. This happens in rehearsal with the traditional use of blocking and gesture.

———

So that's it. I don't think anyone can learn how to make another person's "art," but, hopefully, if you're someone who writes or performs or makes theatre in any way, maybe all this is helpful by simply revealing how one person gets from A to B to C.

At the end of the day, my work is about my taste or style as an artist. It is a function of the way I see things, and so it's about the way I choose to act. Ultimately, it is an argument. The stronger the work, the more convincing my argument. What I make is unique to who I am. It is easy to believe that we are isolated within our skins, within the confines of the time span of our lives, that no one can extend beyond those boundaries. And yet, if an artist can make contact with another sensibility by conjuring his or her perspective on life, that is surely a form of transcendence.

Ultimately, there's no way to really tell you how I actually find any particular arrangement of words, postures, themes, voices. It feels right or it doesn't. But I do look for the "right" arrangement, the configuration that best says what I have to say. And I do discard pieces if they don't feel right. Another way of looking at it is this: I put on stage what I would most like to see if I walked into the theatre.

Eric Bogosian
New York City
February 2002